A Parisian in
BRAZIL

A Parisian in Brazil

THE TRAVEL ACCOUNT OF A FRENCHWOMAN IN NINETEENTH-CENTURY RIO DE JANEIRO

ADÈLE TOUSSAINT-SAMSON
TRANSLATED BY EMMA TOUSSAINT

edited and introduced by June E. Hahner

A Scholarly Resources Inc. Imprint
Wilmington, Delaware

Scholarly Resources Inc.
104 Greenhill Avenue
Wilmington, DE 19805-1897
www.scholarly.com

Library of Congress Cataloging-in-Publication Data

Toussaint-Samson, Mme. (Adèle), b. 1826.
[Parisienne au Brésil. English]
A Parisian in Brazil : the travel account of a
Frenchwoman in nineteenth-century Rio de Janeiro / by
Adèle Toussaint-Samson; translated by Emma Toussaint;
edited and introduced by June E. Hahner.
p. cm. — (Latin American silhouettes)
Includes bibliographical references.
ISBN 0-8420-2854-4 (alk. paper) — ISBN 0-8420-2855-2
(pbk. : alk. paper)
1. Toussaint-Samson, Mme. (Adèle), b. 1826. 2. Brazil
—Description and travel. 3. Brazil—Social life and
customs—19th century. 4. Slavery—Brazil—History—
19th century. 5. Sex role—Brazil—History—19th century.
6. Brazil—Race relations. I. Hahner, June Edith, 1940–
II. Title. III. Series.

F2513 .T78 2001
981'.04—dc21   2001020631

∞ The paper used in this publication meets the minimum
requirements of the American National Standard for per-
manence of paper for printed library materials, Z39.48, 1984.

Acknowledgments

I first made the acquaintance of Adèle Toussaint-Samson more than twenty years ago through the kindness of Mary Karasch, who introduced me to Adèle's account of her sojourn in midnineteenth-century Brazil. Mary Karasch, in turn, had learned of this book from Rollie Poppino. Historical research is often intertwined with friendship, especially in a field that has a relatively small number of practitioners in this country. And I have been very fortunate over the years in this regard. When one of my research trips to Rio de Janeiro coincided with one of Roderick and Jean Barman's in 1998, we talked extensively about Adèle Toussaint-Samson and her book. It is to these good scholars, and good friends, Mary Karasch, Roderick Barman, and Jean Barman, that much is owed.

The staff of the Arquivo Nacional in Rio de Janeiro facilitated my efforts to learn more about Adèle Toussaint-Samson and the places she visited in Brazil. I would like to express my gratitude to the archive's director, Jaime da Silva Antunes, and to Marilda Dias Alves, José Gabriel da Costa Pinto, Maria Isabel Falcão, Sátiro Nunes, and José Luiz Macedo de Faria Santos as well as to Pedro Tortima and Maura Macedo Correia e Costa of the Instituto Histórico e Geográfico Brasileiro; Sonia A. Doyle, head of the Biblioteca Histórico do Itamarati; the staff of the Biblioteca Nacional do Rio de Janeiro; Ben Steinberg and the staff of the Brookline, Massachusetts, Public Library; and the staff of the State University of New York at Albany's library. I wish to thank Miriam Lifchitz Moreira Leite of the Universidade de São Paulo for generously providing me with a Xerox copy of the Portuguese translation of Adèle Toussaint-Samson's travel account. I gratefully acknowledge the Coleção Maria Cecília and Paulo Fontainha Geyer/Museu Imperial, which possesses what seems to be the only surviving copy of the original Portuguese translation, and I wish to thank Sr. Geyer himself for allowing me to consult this volume. Colleagues in Albany, Dan S. White and Robert R. Dykstra, also helped by responding to my queries with information on possible sources in this country and other related matters.

About the Editor

June E. Hahner, professor of history at the State University of New York at Albany, is one of the pioneers of the history of women in Latin America. Her first book on Latin American women, *A Mulher no Brasil*, was published in Rio de Janeiro in 1978. Her other books include *Women through Women's Eyes: Latin American Women in Nineteenth-Century Travel Accounts* (1998); *Emancipating the Female Sex: The Struggle for Women's Rights in Brazil, 1850–1940* (1990); *Poverty and Politics: The Urban Poor in Brazil, 1870–1920* (1986); *Women in Latin American History: Their Lives and Views* (1976; rev. ed., 1980); and *Civilian-Military Relations in Brazil, 1889–1898* (1969).

Contents

Editor's Introduction

June E. Hahner

In the midnineteenth century, Adèle Toussaint-Samson, a high-spirited and enterprising young Parisian, traveled with her husband from France to Brazil, seeking to improve their family fortunes. Like some other foreign visitors to Latin America, she wrote about her experiences, producing one of the best, although long-forgotten, nineteenth-century travel narratives. Adèle Toussaint-Samson's careful account of her more than decade-long stay in Brazil remains a valuable source of insights and information, especially on slavery and gender relations, in that overwhelmingly rural, highly stratified South American society of the 1850s.[1]

The nineteenth century was the period of peak popularity for travel literature. Increasing numbers of foreigners journeyed from Europe and the United States to Latin America, sometimes writing detailed accounts of their trips. Although most of these foreign travelers were men, a small but growing number of women also portrayed the places and people they encountered. Their travel narratives could appeal to a large public, providing readers with both education and vicarious adventure. Travel writing for an expanding market even afforded a living for a few authors and at least the hope of profits for many others, including Adèle Toussaint-Samson. Several women writers, such as Maria Graham and Fanny Calderón de la Barca,[2] not only gained large audiences during their lifetimes but have also maintained their position as important sources on Latin America. Others, such as Adèle Toussaint-Samson, were quickly forgotten, although they too wrote appealing and valuable volumes. These firsthand accounts still possess an immediacy that enables readers to witness closeup Latin American societies and their peoples.

The foreigners who journeyed to Latin America, like those who ventured to Asia or Africa, carried their cultural prejudices and racial, gender, and class biases with them, and these in turn could obstruct their vision. Certainly, the language they used can seem very racist to today's readers. Their observations tended to be based on models of behavior found in their own countries. No matter what their nationality, religion, or location, travel writers, female or male, remained outsiders. Yet as outsiders, portrayers of the "other," travelers tended to note that which was novel or different from things at home and which was accepted by local inhabitants as natural or not worthy of comment. Unlike so many of their subjects, they were literate and sufficiently educated to keep diaries or write letters or narratives. In contrast to many other foreigners, however, Adèle Toussaint-Samson quickly learned the language of her host country, where she lived for a dozen years rather than just visited for a few weeks or months. Nor did she possess the Protestant prejudices exhibited by many writers from Great Britain or the United States. Nevertheless, even though she was a shrewd, attentive observer, not superficial or careless, Adèle could not escape the racist ideologies of the time.

The subordinate position of women in Europe or the United States, particularly in the early nineteenth century, often restricted their opportunities to write and publish, just as it did their ability to travel. Matrimonial restraints, a paucity of legal rights, and circumscribed education all imposed boundaries on female behavior. The treatment that women travelers received differed from that accorded to men. A French man would not have been subjected to the blatant attempts at sexual conquest that Adèle described. Unlike her, many women travelers apparently felt obliged to write primarily about subjects considered suitable for female participation and comment, such as scenic rides, shopping, and street life. Few women travelers ventured into the countryside or described slave life on plantations, as she did. Accounts of subjects considered unseemly for women might not win favor with publishers or the reading public. However, unlike some lesser authors, including many of the more numerous travel writers from the United States or Great Britain, Adèle never feigned reluctance or disavowed intentions of publication in order to conform to contemporary standards of femininity and to prove her modesty.

Although Adèle tells us much about the Brazil of the 1850s, she says relatively little about herself and less about her family. She situates herself as the protagonist of her story, as reaffirmed by the title of her book, relating incidents and situations as an active participant in them. And she displays a sense of social authority when describing the people around her. But she is reticent about many matters that twentieth-century authors, unlike their nineteenth-century female counterparts, might tell us, such as her husband's name and occupation. She never explains precisely when or why they traveled to Brazil or how they supported themselves there for a dozen years. All she tells us about her background, in passing, is that she came from "the artistic centre of Paris" and was "accustomed to listen to the debating of all social, political, literary, and artistic questions in my father's drawing-room," without ever naming him, either.[3] Hence we need to do some historical detective work in an effort to puzzle out some basic facts about her.

Through a bibliographical search we learn that Adèle Toussaint-Samson was the daughter of Joseph-Isidore Samson (1793–1871), renowned actor, teacher, and playwright and the doyen of the Comédie Française, for she wrote an introduction to his *Mémoires*.[4] However, in that introduction she said nothing about herself. During the same period in the early 1880s when that book appeared, she also published a volume of sketches and a brief comedy as well as her account of her Brazilian sojourn. Years earlier she had published two books of poetry, one prior to her marriage.[5] Thus we can understand why in her Brazilian narrative she positioned herself as a Parisian from an intellectual family. Pride in her father and her family background no doubt explains her use of Toussaint-Samson as her surname, rather than following the more common practice of placing the maiden name before the husband's surname. We also see why she could move easily in Brazil's elite social circles. For educated, European-oriented Brazilians, France occupied a position of cultural preeminence, with Paris seen as the capital of civilization.

The name of Adèle Toussaint-Samson's husband proved more complicated to determine than that of her father. In 1891 her 1883 travel account of Brazil appeared in the United States in a translation by Emma Toussaint. From the book's new dedication by Emma, we learn that she was Adèle's daughter, presumably born after her parents' return to France; in her book Adèle had mentioned a young son, Paul, who traveled with his parents to Brazil, and a son, Maurice, born in Brazil, but no daughter. We also learn from Emma's dedication that although her mother, Adèle, was deceased by the time of writing, in 1890, Emma's father, that is, Adèle's husband, still lived. (While we do not know the precise date of Adèle's death, which possibly occurred around 1885, library catalogs give her birth date as 1826.) Since Emma's dedication also included a location, Aspinwall Avenue in Brookline, a Boston suburb, another line of investigation opened up. Through the help and efforts of librarians at the Brookline Public Library, which contains copies, found nowhere else, of the local city directory, the *Blue Book of Brookline*, going back to its beginnings in 1885, the names of residents on that street could be traced. That 1885 directory listed Winand J. Toussaint as living at 203 Aspinwall Avenue. Emma's name only appears for the first time in the 1893 directory, despite her having given Aspinwall Avenue as her address in her 1890 dedication to Adèle's book. The 1904 directory contains only Emma's name, not Winand's. A request to the Massachusetts State Archives for death records produced a copy of his death certificate, stating that Winand W. J. Toussaint, a widower, who had been born in Liège, Belgium, died in Brookline on February 10, 1904, aged 77 years, 4 months, and 2 days. (No will was filed with the county.)

Even though Winand Toussaint's death certificate confirmed Emma as his daughter, it raised another question or, rather, pointed to an apparent discrepancy. The only information Adèle had given about her husband was in passing; when relating an incident concerning a slave's punishment, she mentioned that he had been "born in Brazil, of French parents, spoke Portuguese as his native language."[6] In parts of Europe, national borders and sentiments were more fluid in the early nineteenth century than they would be later. The Bishopric of Liège had been part of the Austrian Netherlands, but, with the French Revolution, Liège passed into French hands and then was assigned to the Netherlands by the Congress of Vienna in 1815. Belgium only became a nation in 1830, several years after Winand Toussaint's birth, and many of its French-speaking inhabitants, the Walloons (and Liège lies in Wallonia), continued to think of themselves as French in culture if not in nationality. Winand probably did also, but his daughter, when providing information for an official death certificate in the early twentieth century, used contemporary political divisions. Perhaps too, in her account, Adèle located her husband's birthplace in Brazil to heighten the literary effect, rather than saying that he came to Brazil as a very young child and grew up there.

Attempts to determine how the Toussaints made their living while in Brazil—and whether they grew rich, as they had hoped—raise additional questions, although the Toussaints must have earned an income sufficient to enable Adèle to make the five long transatlantic voyages back to France she refers to in the introduction to her book. In the *Brookline Directory* in the 1890s and in the 1900 manuscript census of Massachusetts, Winand Toussaint is listed as an architect.[7] (The *Brookline Directory* had earlier listed him as a furniture manufacturer and then as a designer at the Emerson Piano Factory of Boston.[8]) But no Toussaint is found among the architects listed in the *Almanak Laemmert* for Rio de Janeiro during the 1850s, nor are any Toussaints mentioned among the city's piano or furniture manufacturers. However, a Júlio Toussaint is included among the dance instructors as well as a Madame Toussaint, residing at the same address, found among the foreign language instructors during that decade. According to the records of the imperial household, a Jules Toussaint was employed as dance instructor to the Princess Isabel, daughter and heir of Emperor Pedro II, and her sister from 1857 to 1863,[9] a distinction Júlio Toussaint added to his listing in the *Almanak*

Laemmert, and which probably helped him acquire more pupils. Is this Júlio/Jules Toussaint the same person as Winand Toussaint? Certainly Júlio, or even Jules, would be a far easier first name for Brazilians to pronounce than Winand. Or could he be the mysterious uncle "in America" whom Adèle mentioned for the first and only time at the beginning of her book? We cannot be sure. Dating the Toussaints' sojourn in Brazil also proved less than certain. The imperial government's *entrada de estrangeiros*, the exit rather than the entrance records, might have noted dates for family members. But the Arquivo Nacional do Rio de Janeiro, Brazil's national archive, does not have these records for the 1840s, 1850s, and 1860s. Therefore, we must mine Adèle's book. Although she declines to tell us when she first sailed from France to Brazil, she provides some information that enables us to calculate the probable date as late 1849. When she writes about her experience with yellow fever, to which foreigners such as herself proved most susceptible, she declares that she and her husband took sick three months after their arrival in Rio de Janeiro and also that this was the first time Brazil had suffered harshly from this frightful disease. We know that even though yellow fever had raged in areas of seventeenth-century Brazil, the disease was then confined to local outbreaks; it did not return in epidemic proportions until 1849, when yellow fever attacked Rio de Janeiro in December of that year. The date of the Toussaints' return to France seems easier to calculate, since Adèle stated that the family lived in Brazil for twelve years, in which case they would have departed around 1862.

The problem of dating the Toussaints' sojourn in Rio de Janeiro and the question of what Adèle's husband did in that city intersect. If Winand Toussaint is Júlio/Jules Toussaint, then he appears to have been in Rio prior to

1849, for the *Almanak Laemmert* first lists Júlio Toussaint in 1848, and continues to list him every year until 1870. "Madame Toussaint," however, is only found in the 1851 to 1859 issues of the almanac. Could Winand Toussaint have first set himself up as a dance instructor before taking his family from France to Brazil? Or did the family's first encounter with yellow fever occur more than three months after their arrival, so dramatically depicted in Adèle's book? Was the *Almanak Laemmert* always updated or could it publish listings of people after they ceased practicing their professions? The imperial household's records contain a letter acknowledging Jules Toussaint's departure from its service in 1863.[10]

Adèle Toussaint-Samson did have contact with the imperial family. In her book, she tells us that she was twice admitted to intimate soirées given by the emperor's daughters. Years later, when living in Passy, an upper-class suburb of Paris, she wrote Emperor Pedro II, sending him one of her books while thanking him for kindnesses shown her and her husband.[11] A book of hers inscribed to Dom Pedro's daughter and heir, Isabel, would be retained by the princess until, much later, Isabel's husband, the Conde d'Eu, donated a large book collection that became the historical library of Itamaratí Palace, Brazil's Foreign Ministry

To establish the dates of the Toussaints' sojourn is not the same as determining when, during those dozen years, particular incidents occurred, let alone when Adèle wrote her account of them. In the Preface, she indicates that she wrote her "sketches" or "souvenirs" in France some time before her book's publication date of 1883, based on notes taken in Brazil. We can see that she updated parts of the book's final section, since she refers to events that occurred after her final departure such as the Paraguayan War (1864–1870), performances at Rio's Théâtre Lyrique, which only opened in the mid-1860s, and two trips by Emperor Pedro II to Europe that included France, undertaken in the 1870s. No doubt she sought to reflect changes that had transpired in the expanding and modernizing city of Rio de Janeiro since her initial arrival in the middle of the nineteenth century.

At that time, foreign travelers faced more danger, difficulty, and delay en route than would later visitors to Latin America. When Adèle, her husband, and young son set sail on a clipper ship from Le Havre to Rio de Janeiro around 1849, the age of steam travel had not really begun and the Atlantic passage was still slow, difficult, and dangerous. Europe and Brazil would not be linked by regularly scheduled steamships until 1851, when the Royal Mail Steam Packet Company instituted service from Southampton to Rio de Janeiro, strengthening Great Britain's preeminent commercial position in Brazil. Only after sailing ships were replaced by faster, cheaper, and safer steamships would increasing numbers of both foreign visitors and poor immigrants head across the Atlantic, as international trade, commerce, and investment continued to expand.

The empire of Brazil in which the Toussaints lived in the midnineteenth century was comprised of only seven million people scattered across three million square miles of the eastern half of South America. A highly stratified society with an economy dependent on slave labor, Brazil appeared backward in the eyes of visiting Europeans. The majority of its racially and ethnically diverse population remained concentrated on the coast, living on the land and farming with crude techniques. Most towns seemed sleepy places with muddy streets frequented by pack mules, pigs, and chickens, although they also served as social, religious, and market centers for nearby areas. Methods of transportation were rudimentary and manufacturing industries practically nonexistent.

Brazil had made the transition from Portuguese colony to independent empire in a gradual, largely peaceful fashion. Unlike Spain's empire in America, Portugal's did not disintegrate into a series of independent nations but instead evolved into one country, Brazil. The presence of members of Portugal's royal family after the court's arrival in Rio de Janeiro in 1808, following the Napoleonic invasion of the Iberian Peninsula, lent legitimacy to the process. And the monarchy served as a unifier. Brazil would remain an independent monarchy, unique in the New World, from 1822, the official date of independence, until 1889, when a republic would be declared.

Following the forced abdication in 1831 of Pedro I, Brazil's first emperor and the son of João VI of Portugal, the crown devolved to Pedro's infant son, the Brazilian-born and -raised Pedro II. By the time the Toussaints arrived in Rio in the middle of the nineteenth century, Pedro II was ruling in his own stead. This fragmented, far-flung empire, with its overwhelmingly illiterate, racially diverse population, had entered into a period of stability and order, with prosperity and growth, at least for the elites.

Politics during the empire proved highly personal in nature and were marked by shifting coalitions of factions and individuals within the upper classes. Personalism and clientelism marked relations among members of the upper strata of society just as it did their dealings with the lower orders. Within the small political community, personal relationships, distinctions, and interests rather than ideologies guided decision making. The parties lacked national organization and popularity as well as political philosphies. Their major concern remained the control of local patronage and power so as to secure their places in the central government. The vast authority of the emperor further personalized imperial politics. He could veto legislation, dissolve at will the Chamber of Deputies, and make war or peace as well as appoint ministers of state, members of the Senate, presidents of the provinces, and other major officials. Patient and persevering, generally conservative, well-educated but perhaps lacking in imagination, Pedro II helped provide the elites with an efficient government reflective of their needs and kept competing political interests content. This tall, handsome emperor with his serious and calm demeanor and reputation for integrity and impartiality enjoyed great personal prestige at home and abroad, commanding the respect of both his subjects and visiting foreigners.

The imperial capital of Rio de Janeiro, where the Toussaint family landed, served as Brazil's major commercial, financial, administrative, and transportation center, based on the cultivation and exportation of coffee and the importation and distribution of both necessities and luxury items, including the latest European fads and notions. The seat of national power and the country's economic, cultural, and intellectual leader, Rio had over 200,000 inhabitants around 1850, making it the largest city in South America. The Rua Direita, described by Adèle in detail, was the city's principal artery, running the length of the old colonial section of the city and paralleling the waterfront where visitors disembarked.

During the years she lived in Brazil, the country enjoyed political stability and increasing prosperity for the elites, especially in the provinces of Rio de Janeiro and São Paulo. The suppression of the African slave trade in 1850 released capital for internal investments but the colonial dependence on exports continued. Commerce expanded. Foreign demand for coffee grew. By the 1850s and 1860s, new forms of communication and transportation such as the railroad, steamship, and electronic telegraph began to link the country together as never before, altering the Brazil that Adèle had first encountered. During this period, Rio itself experienced a series of municipal improvements, which accelerated as the century progressed. Gas lighting first appeared in Rio in 1854, replacing whale oil on a few downtown streets. The telegraph arrived in 1854. In 1856 the omnibus made its appearance, to be followed in 1868 by the *bondes*, mule-drawn streetcars on rails. New railroads edged northward from Rio, beginning with the Estrada de Ferro Dom Pedro Segundo, later called the Central do Brasil, whose first section was completed in 1858. These improvements in urban transportation accelerated the rate of Rio's growth, both in physical area and in population size, and served the needs of the country's export-oriented economy.

African slavery provided the foundation of Brazil's export economy. Some of the densest slave concentrations were found on the historic sugar coast of the Northeast, in the Province of Rio de Janeiro, and, later, in the coffee-producing Province of São Paulo. Foreign visitors to Rio de Janeiro in the midnineteenth century compared the Brazilian capital to an African city, with almost 40 percent of its population enslaved. After 1850 and the end of the slave trade from Africa, and then the steady increase in European immigration, the number of slaves and the percentage of enslaved among Rio's population would decline steadily, until the final abolition of slavery in 1888.

Although all slaves remained "private property," individuals' specific situations and experiences differed greatly. Not just gender but race, occupation, and location also helped to determine many aspects of their lives. However, while some scholars stress slaves' resistance and adaptation, others emphasize the privations suffered by them. Certainly, female slaves, unlike free women, might be forcibly separated from their children and even obliged to serve as wet nurses to their owners' offspring. Slave women remained subject to sexual violence and the advances of their masters. Yet some slaves, particularly in the cities, succeeded in constructing limited family or personal lives, even though ultimate control remained in their masters' hands. Urban slave women sometimes enjoyed considerable personal freedom, going about the city (with their masters' permission) selling food they prepared or fruits and vegetables they raised, while their mistresses generally remained cloistered at home, shielded from the perceived vulgarities or dangers of the street, as we can see in Adèle's narrative. However, most slaves in Brazil, as in other countries, were field hands, not street sellers or domestic servants, and both men and women engaged in harsh physical labor on the plantations.

As a European woman of the midnineteenth century, Adèle abhorred slavery and described its cruelties while also displaying her strong distaste for aspects of the slaves' appearance, behavior, and imputed morality. She expressed what today would be seen as strong racial prejudices, but views that were typical of Europeans of her time. But her descriptions of slave life, especially her account of a visit to a *fazenda*, or plantation, in the Province of Rio de Janeiro owned by a friend of her husband's, included detailed information on slaves' diet and treatment rarely provided by either Brazilians or foreign travelers.

Although Adèle tells us neither the exact time nor place of that visit, nor the complete name of her host,

"Senhor P__," we can seek them out. Since she informs us that her eldest son was seven years old when they journeyed to that *fazenda*, and she had earlier given his age as eighteen months when yellow fever arrived in Rio de Janeiro, we can calculate the date of the plantation visit as most likely 1855. This year is supported by her statement concerning the recent establishment of an American-owned cotton mill in Santo Aleixo, since we know that factory to have started around 1850.

A search through the collections of old maps and almanacs of the Province of Rio de Janeiro found in Brazil's Arquivo Nacional do Rio de Janeiro produced the most probable owner and location of the Fazenda São José: Polycarpo José Alves de Azevedo in the parish of Nossa Senhora da Ajuda da Guapymerim in the municipality of Majé. That municipality lay at the head of the Bay of Guanabara, where the recently introduced steamer from Rio that Adèle's family had taken would land, and it included Santo Aleixo and its cotton mill. Old maps show a nearby plantation owned by P. Alves. According to the *Almanak Laemmert* of 1856, Colonel Alves de Azevedo, who died in 1861, served as a member of the municipal council and held the honors of the Order of Our Lord Jesus Christ and the Order of the Rose. The Viscondessa de P__G__, owner of a nearby plantation where the Toussaints spent a night, no doubt was the Viscondessa da Praia Grande.[12] Certainly, Adèle and her husband moved easily in upper-class circles in Brazil. The wealthy plantation owner of the *fazenda* São José later asked her to be godmother to one of his children, thus establishing the close relationship of co-parenthood between them.

Conscious of herself as a Parisian, not just a cultured Frenchwoman, Adèle commented pointedly on gender relations among Brazilians as well as on the behavior of Brazilian males toward foreign females. However, she made no mention of the received opinion of the period in Brazil concerning the sexual availability of most Frenchwomen or the claim to be French by many high-class prostitutes. Adèle detailed her own dealings with Brazilian women, from white upper-class females to maltreated slaves. She even began her book with advice to foreign women facing the social snares of crossing the Atlantic alone at a time when few respectable women traveled without a male escort.

Like some male foreign travelers, Adèle portrayed upper-class Brazilian women as being treated like dolls by their husbands, but she also noted their ability to run large households. However, unlike many other foreigners who commented on those women's apparent laziness, she understood that accepted patterns of behavior required them to appear calm and carefree before guests, never revealing the weight of their domestic obligations. She appreciated the Brazilians' hospitality and openness as well as their country's sunshine and natural beauty, and she ended her book with a nostalgic longing to see once more the Brazil she had known. Today, we, too, can view that South American nation of one hundred and fifty years ago through the eyes of this intelligent, spirited, and perceptive Parisian.

Notes

1. Adèle Toussaint-Samson's account appeared in both France and Brazil in 1883 and in the United States in 1891: *Une Parisienne au Brésil* (Paris: Paul Ollendorff, 1883); *Viagem de uma Parisiense ao Brasil. Estudo e crítica dos costumes brasileiros*, trans. Antonio Estevão da Costa e Cunha (Rio de Janeiro: Typ. de J. Villeneuve & C., 1883); and *A Parisian in Brazil*, trans. Emma Toussaint (Boston: James H. Earle, 1891). A comparison of the English translation with the French original shows no major changes or deletions, although the section of the story at the end of Part II concerning a wife-murderer in Rio that indicated that the actress in question did actually become the mistress of her supposed lover was eliminated, as was a later description of slave child-

birth and of miscegenation; such changes perhaps reflect a difference in anticipated readers' reactions and proprieties in France and in the United States. However, Portuguese names and words that were properly spelt in the French edition are often incorrect in the English version. U.S. publishers, unlike Garnier in Paris, did not employ a Portuguese-speaking proofreader. For the U.S. edition, the photographs in the French edition were replaced by engravings made from those photographs, while the Brazilian edition contains no illustrations whatsoever. The only known existing copy of the Portuguese-language edition of Adèle Toussaint-Samson's account seems to be that found in the Coleção Maria Cecília and Paulo Fontainha Geyer/Museu Imperial in Rio. The copy of the Portuguese-language edition once found in the Biblioteca Nacional do Rio de Janeiro, according to Paulo Berger, *Bibliografia do Rio de Janeiro de viajantes e autores estrangeiros, 1531–1900* (Rio de Janeiro: Livraria São José, 1964), is no longer even listed in the library's card catalog. The Portuguese-language edition of Adèle Toussaint-Samson's book, which misspells her name as Toussaint-Simon, omitted the Preface in which she gave her reasons for writing the book and the difficulties she encountered in getting it published, as well as the appendix containing several Brazilian poems. This translation was also published as a serial in the March 14, 16, 21, 23, 24, and 25, 1883, issues of the *Jornal do Comércio* in Rio de Janeiro. In several rather pedantic footnotes added to this edition, the translator, Antonio Estevão da Costa e Cunha—whose name is given in the *Jornal do Comércio* but not in the book—a primary schoolteacher and author of a Portuguese grammar book and other works intended for classroom use (Augusto Victorino Alves Sacramento Blake, *Diccionario Bibliografico Brasileiro*, 7 vols. ([Rio de Janeiro: Typ. Nacional, 1883–1902], I, 156), takes pains to criticize Adèle Toussaint's knowledge of Brazil. A new Portuguese translation of her travel account is scheduled to be published by Editora Mulheres of Florianópolis in 2002.

2. Maria Dundas Graham (Lady Callcott), *Journal of a Voyage to Brazil, and Residence There, During Part of the Years 1821, 1822, 1823* (London: Longman, Hurst, Rees, Orme, Brown, and Green, and J. Murray, 1824), and *Journal of a Residence in Chile During the Year 1822 and a Voyage from Chile to Brazil in 1823* (London: Longman, Hurst, Rees, Orme, Brown, and Green, and J. Murray, 1824); Frances Calderón de la Barca, *Life in Mexico During a Residence of Two Years in That Country* (Boston: Little, Brown and Co., 1843).

3. Toussaint-Samson, *A Parisian in Brazil*, 134 (this volume, p. 89).

4. Joseph-Isidore Samson, *Mémoires de Samson de la Comèdie Française* (Paris: Paul Ollendorff, 1882).

5. *Les Chemins de la Vie, études de moeurs* (Paris: E. Dentu, 1881); *La Comtesse Diane, comédie en 1 acte* (Paris: Imp. Vve. Edouard Vert, 1884); *Epaves, sourires et larmes, poésies de Mme. Toussaint, née Samson* (Paris: E. Dentu, 1870); *Poésies de Mlle. Adèle Samson* (Paris: Jules-Juteau, 1843).

6. Toussaint-Samson, *A Parisian in Brazil*, 59 (this volume, p. 44).

7. 1900 Census. Decennial Population Schedule. Norfolk County, Mass. T 623, roll 669. While historians always seek to question their sources, they may sometimes assume certain sources to be more reliable than others, and perhaps trust censuses too much. The attempt to learn more about Adèle Toussaint-Samson's husband shows how some census data can be inaccurate. Winand Toussaint's 1900 entry lists his birthplace as Germany and that of his daughter Emma's mother, that is, Adèle, the proud Parisian, as Germany also.

8. Winand Toussaint first appears in the 1877–78 edition of the *Brookline Directory*. By the 1883–84 directory he is working for the Emerson Piano Factory, and in the 1890s he is listed as an architect. In 1881, Adèle Toussaint-Samson appears to have been residing in the Parisian suburb of Passy, since the letter she wrote to D. Pedro II in 1881 was sent from there.

9. Luiz Pedreira do Couto Ferraz to Paulo Barbosa da Silva, Rio de Janeiro, February 3, 1857, Arquivo Nacional, Rio de Janeiro, Casa Imperial, Cx. 15, Pac. 2, Doc. 35; Paulo Barbosa da Silva to Marquez de Olinda, September 30, 1863, Arquivo Nacional, Casa Imperial, Cx. 16, Pac. 2, Doc. 26. Professor Roderick Barman of the University of British Columbia initially called my attention to the fact that a Jules Toussaint was mentioned as imperial dance instructor in Lourenço Luiz Lacombe, *Isabel. A Princesa Redentora* (Petrópolis: Instituto Histórico de Petrópolis, 1989), 88.

10. Paulo Barbosa da Silva to Marquez de Olinda, September 30, 1863, Arquivo Nacional, Casa Imperial, Cx. 16, Pac. 2, Doc. 26.

11. Adèle Toussaint to Pedro II, Passy, April 19, 1881, Biblioteca Nacional do Rio de Janeiro, Divisão de Manuscritos, 1-35.9.32 (Coleção Teresa Cristina Maria). Roderick Barman kindly called my attention to this letter.

12. *Almanak administrativo, mercantil e industrial da Corte e provincia do Rio de Janeiro para o ano de 1856* (Rio de Janeiro: Eduardo e Henrique Laemmert, 1856), 182, 187.

A

PARISIAN IN BRAZIL

TRANSLATED FROM THE FRENCH OF

MME. TOUSSAINT-SAMSON

BY

EMMA TOUSSAINT

WITH ORIGINAL ILLUSTRATIONS

BOSTON
JAMES H. EARLE, Publisher
178 Washington Street
1891

TO

Monsieur Louis Jacolliot*

While you are musing on the shores of the ocean, or in your charming Indian villa, oblivious of Paris and the Parisians, I, my dear friend, frequently think of the indefatigable traveller, of the passionate admirer of India, whose accounts have had such success, and which have kept me spellbound whole evenings, and it is to give him a proof of my strong fellow-feeling that I beg him to accept the dedication of this little volume, which he frequently urged me to finish.

May he, in reading it, not repent too deeply his imprudent counsel!

AD. TOUSSAINT-SAMSON

*Louis Jacolliot (1837–1890) was the author of numerous books on travel as well as on mythology and religion, focusing on India.—Ed.

The translation of this book is a loving tribute to its authoress. The incentive to work: the memory of my dear mother, with the constant encouragement of my father.

EMMA TOUSSAINT

ASPINWALL AVE., BROOKLINE, 1890

Contents

Preface

$\mathcal{I}$f it has ever happened, reader, that you have been once in your life in pursuit of a publisher, I can feel assured of your sympathy, and can begin the history of this book. When I returned from Brazil some years ago, bringing from that country and its inhabitants notes gathered during my long sojourn at Rio Janeiro, which, in default of other merit, had at least that of the most scrupulous veracity, and to which were added the photographs of the principal churches and public places of the capital of Brazil, likewise the types of Indians, mulattoes, and negroes taken from life, I imagined that all this would offer some interest to my compatriots, and that I could easily have it published. I had completely forgotten the usages and customs of my native land, as you will easily see. I wrote, to begin with, to the principal editor of one of our leading illustrated papers, to whom I was not unknown, offering him my "Sketches of Brazil." His reply was not tardy in coming: "There was no need of my troubling to send him my manuscript," he wrote, "because he possessed so many documents on South America, and had already published so many things upon Brazil, that the subject seemed exhausted to him."

I had, fortunately, the complete file of the paper up to that evening. I skipped eagerly to the index for Brazil, which referred me to three articles, of twenty or thirty lines each, treating of the subject in question. The first gave the date of the discovery of America, likewise the name of the first navigators who took possession of Brazil. This was already quite spicy, you will admit, and altogether new, above all.

In the second article, which placarded the pretension of being a study of the habits of South Americans, the author, who had drawn his knowledge out of the accounts of travellers buried since half a century, taught me, who had lived twelve years in that country, a fact of which I was totally ignorant, which was to say, that the inhabitants of Rio Janeiro never paid their calls but in full dress, short breeches, and three-cornered hats under their arms. Those of the interior, according to him, did not go out to go to church but upon large chariots of two wooden wheels, and the engraving which accompanied the text represented in effect the above-mentioned chariot, surmounted by a sort of dais, under which some women dressed in Spanish fashion were seated, with their legs dangling, while the negroes, dressed also in the fashion of the guerillas, were driving the team of oxen; all this scene was passing in a naked and barren landscape, where one could see only rocks and sand.

Now in Brazil the rocks even are covered with the most luxuriant vegetation. The walls of the habitations and the roofs are loaded with creeping plants. All this was therefore absolutely fanciful.

If there ever had been any truth in the costumes of the Brazilians depicted, it might date back to sixty years ago at least. Still, it seems that information of such freshness was amply sufficient to the Brazilian, who showed himself perfectly satisfied.

Seeing this, I was obliged to bow, and address myself to another illustrated paper, in which I had already published several things. This was quite a different matter.

"Are there tigers, serpents, missionaries eaten by savages, in what you bring me?"

Such was the director's first question.

"My goodness! no," I replied meekly. "I come to offer you a sketch of the habits and customs of a country which I have lived in twelve years; I tell what I have seen, and don't invent anything."

"So much the worse," he replied; "it's useless then to leave me your manuscript. We have recently published a novel whose scene is laid in Brazil, and which has had great success; oncas, jaguars, boa-constrictors, and savages,—nothing was missing; it was very exciting."

"I don't doubt it; but without doubt the author had travelled in the interior and explored the whole country."

"Not the least in the world," laughingly continued the director of the paper. "The author, that's I. I had helped myself from several accounts, more or less true, on America, and had then sewn my fable. What is necessary before all is to amuse the reader."

"But may one not hope to interest him, at least, with a true painting?"

"No: he needs, first of all, emotions."

"Then serve him tigers; as for me, I am grieved that I have not even the smallest one to offer you." And thereupon I left, carrying back for the second time my manuscript in its virgin purity.

"Since the papers refuse my 'Souvenirs of Brazil,' " thought I, "then let me offer them to the public in book form."

Therefore I gathered up my courage one day and went in search of an editor. As I was about to speak, to explain what I had brought—"Before all," speaking to me, "how many pages will it make?"

"About two hundred and fifty, I think."

"What ! you suppose? you are not sure. That is not much, madam," he answered in a doctoral tone; "even with the engravings, it amounts to little; we certainly should have to have one hundred pages more."

"I should rather fear, perhaps, to add trifling details. I have chosen in my Souvenirs that which I thought interesting."

"No matter! can't you embellish?"

"I don't want to embellish."

"Then stretch the matter, stretch it."

"I desire still less to stretch, having always thought that one of the principal merits of style was conciseness."

"That has something to do with it, really. One can see you are no longer in the swim, madam. Here is the manner in which our fashionable authors work nowadays: They know that a volume is generally composed of at least some three hundred pages, twenty-four lines each. What do they do? They begin by dividing the number of pages of twenty-four lines, of which each must give so many words apiece; then they make it their duty each day to fill out, say, fifteen or twenty pages, according to their more or less facility of work; if the subject has more, they cut it, if it has less, they stretch it; and in this way, madam, they come up to the day and hour, and do not give their editors neither a word more nor less than was stipulated for."

"You open up new vistas before me, monsieur; nothing could seem better."

"Now, isn't that so? We live in a practical age. And your title?"

"Dear me, monsieur, I don't know yet; I had just simply taken 'Souvenirs of Brazil, by a Parisienne.' "

"Impossible, madam, impossible! Who would read that? The title is everything! What would you say to a drama in the virgin forests?"

"But, monsieur, I would say that my work does not enclose, unfortunately, the smallest drama in the virgin forests."

"That's no reason; the title, madam, the title: there is everything in that! Bring me three hundred pages and a good title, and we will manage it without my being obliged to read your manuscript. Just think about it."

"I'll certainly think about it. All you want is three hundred pages and a title; that's it, isn't it? *Au revoir*, monsieur."

A second editor showed me a mountain of manuscripts, accumulated in a large room. "I must read all that before thinking of you," he said. "Come around in a year."

At last, a third one, to whom I had been warmly recommended, decided to intrust my manuscript to one of his examiners, who declared in his report that my work was not in the tone of publication which they issued, but that its style was amiable. I was a woman: they could not allow me more; that was already doing me a great honor.

I then recalled in my mind all that had been told me. The one found the Brazilians of to-day like those of 1809; the other asked for tigers and anthropophagi; the third one only wanted a title and pages; the fourth one put me off forever; and finally the last, the only one who had read me, baptized my style as "amiable." It was the first time that this epithet had been given it. Until then it had been acknowledged, on the contrary, as having qualities and defects entirely opposed. What to do then? Give up producing my "Sketches of Brazil," since my compatriots were absolutely unwilling to have the real truth, and that I certainly was unwilling to laugh at them.

"Let's lock all this up in my bureau," said I to myself, "and talk about it no more." Still, in the mean while, the Emperor of Brazil having come to Paris, I wished to prove to what degree all that I had written was true, since I did not fear to publish it at the very moment when Dom Pedro II was among us. I wrote, therefore, to Villemessant, to ask him if he would publish in the *Figaro* a fragment of my souvenirs which had a sketch of the Emperor and his whole family.

He thought it would be exactly the thing, and gave me the hospitality of his paper, as he had done already several times, in remunerating me largely. But then, behold quite a different story! The whole Brazilian colony residing at Paris rises up and declares it does not at all find my style amiable. I have said that the Brazilian race was degenerate: it is monstrous! It seems, on the contrary, it can wrestle in strength and greatness with the most robust nations of the North. I have pretended that the Brazilian was indolent: nothing is more false! I am assured that he is full of energy. I have announced he was proud: a crazy general rises up against this affirmation, and all the papers of Rio Janeiro confound me. The Emperor is appealed to, who, being the most liberal of all his subjects, does not find that there is reason to be stirred up. "For," he adds, "nations, as well as individuals, cannot judge themselves."

In short, I have praised as well as blamed a nation congenial to me, and, above all, have not wished to exaggerate anything.

When a Brazilian is represented to us, one is in the habit of making him [into] a redskin with jewels on all fingers, and the manners of a savage or monkey. I have wished he should be correctly known. I have shown him as he is,—intelligent, hospitable, very good in his family, and having progressed more in twenty years than any other nation in half a century. May he therefore permit me to tell him his defects as well as his virtues, so that the impartiality of my judgment may give that judgment all its value. May he know how to listen to truth: it is the first sign of moral strength.

And now, what must I think of my style? Is it really so amiable as that gentleman said, or is it absolutely not so, as the Brazilians pretend? It is for the public to give me its opinion, and its final judgment whether I was right in drawing out this book from the bottom of my bureau, where I had relegated it, and in hoping that these sketches upon the Brazilian habits and customs, absolutely true, may have some interest for my compatriots. I wish it, and ask also the Brazilians to receive them well; for, whatever they may think, they have been written by an impartial but friendly pen.

AD. TOUSSAINT

Part I
Life on Board

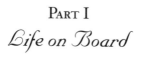

We had an uncle in America, and not of America, which is quite a different thing; nevertheless, this good uncle having made quite a nice fortune in Brazil, we likewise got the idea of trying our fortunes. In ten years, we were told, we ought to be rich. Ten years of exile,—that certainly was something; but the country was so beautiful, and we would return so young still.

There were many hesitations on my part, many tears shed; then, finally, we formed our resolution, and after having embraced parents and friends, we got into the train. We were bound for Havre, where we were to embark for South America.

When we were near arriving at the Havre station, I perceived in the distance all those tall masts, pressed one against the other, which seemed a forest upon the sea. My heart stood still, and I understood by how many ties the father-land was dear to me.

However, the die had been cast: we must go to the end.

The clipper "La Normandie," which was to sail for Rio de Janeiro, and on which our state-rooms were engaged, was swinging restlessly at anchor, like a horse pawing the ground, before starting. She was a fine vessel, whose immense sails would soon cause her to be cutting the waves like a bird through the air. My husband asked me if I would not like to visit her before our departure, which was set for the following morning. I consented, and ascended with him the steps, which all ships have at their sides when anchored.

On the quarter-deck stood the officers of the ship, who came to salute us, and one of whom offered to show us his ship, "La Normandie."

Really, there was nothing he failed to show us: from the quarter-deck, with its immense hen-coops filled with all kinds of fowl, to the bow of the vessel, where the crew sleep, amidst monkeys, parrots, and birds of all kinds; from the pantry, with its long rows of cups, glasses, and plates, so well arranged that the smallest space is utilized, to the very top of the cabin, the steerage even; we saw everything, and that which I inspected with the most attention was the room, that is to say, what must be henceforth for me drawing-room, dining-room, and study.

As for our state-room, when I saw those two elevated frames, from which a little mattress twenty-four inches in width, placed on a board between two other boards, formed all the bed, I thought it would be impossible to ever get any rest, and I was not mistaken.

A cow was installed in a little compartment of the prow where some sheep were already confined. Legs of mutton and hams were hanging from the rigging. The pantry and cupboards were filled with preserves of all kinds. The lockers on both sides of the vessel were being filled with vegetables and fruits, which the peasants were bringing. This removed our fear, certainly, on the question of food.

We returned to the hotel in silence, my husband and I, so lost in thought by the grave resolution which we had taken that we dared not exchange a word on the subject. What distressed me most was my child, for I was taking with me my eldest son, whom I was then nursing, and I was asking myself with anxiety how nurse and nursling would endure such a long voyage. I did not close an eye all night, and the next day, at eight o'clock in the morning, we were on board "La Normandie." Each passenger soon arrived with his baggage, which had to be taken down between decks by means of a tackle. Water was being supplied, coal was being put in, provisions were received; there was a noise, a confusion, an incredible racket. Many friends and relatives accompanied the travellers until the last moment, so that one heard only these words: "You'll write me just as soon as you have arrived." "Give me your address as quickly as possible." "Do not forget me." "*Bon voyage.*" "Return to us with riches." "May God keep you!" And during the half-hour which preceded our departure it was nothing but embraces, tears, sobs, mingled with the yells of the sailors, the orders of the officers, the grating noise of the tackle, and the dull murmur of the waves as they beat against the sides of the vessel.

Meanwhile, the boatswain's whistle had resounded: it was the signal of departure; separation must take place.

The boats approach, friends part, the anchor is raised, the sails swell. Good by, parents, friends, father-land! The handkerchiefs still wave a little while, the pier vanishes in the mist, and the shores of France are effaced in their turn; then nothing more, nothing but the heavens and seas in the horizon. Nearly all the passengers had remained on deck,—eyes moist, heart oppressed,—lost in their thoughts (the larger number), as long as their eyes could distinguish in the distance even but a vague outline of their father-land.

But all at once the heavens became overcast, the wind arose, hailstones appeared, and the rolling began. The countenances paled. My right-hand neighbor leaned forward on the rail of the vessel with significant shrugs; the lady on my left was descending to her room, scarcely able to hold up; a passenger, enveloped in his ulster,* was stretched on the quarter-deck like a lifeless mass; another was walking the deck at a great pace; a dude was trying to smoke, and laugh with the officers, but, alas! soon our hero began to totter, threw away his cigar, asked for a glass of Madeira, which he swallowed with one draught,

*A long, loose, heavy overcoat—Ed.

and trying to keep up a smiling countenance to the last. Useless struggle! The Madeira went to rejoin the cigar. It was then that the cabin-boy began to come up and go down without stopping: it was significant.

One must have a strong stomach to resist all this; further could I only keep up my courage while filling my lungs with invigorating sea air, which was blowing full in my face. But the wind becoming too high, I was forced to leave the deck and go down in the cabin, where a most picturesque sight met my gaze. Men were stretched on the end settees, some half asleep, others holding their heads in their hands, while the most courageous were walking the cabin at a great pace, pushed by the rolling at one time to the right, at another to the left. From each cabin were heard, in the midst of hiccoughs and groans, these words incessantly, "Cabin-boy! cabin-boy!" and the poor child, called thus from all sides, gave himself up to a continual taking and leaving of wash-bowls, which, we must acknowledge, was totally devoid of poetry.

In the midst of all this, the dinner-bell had rung. The captain took his place at the head of the table, the first mate in the centre, and the purser at the foot. Hardly ever are the ladies at table on the first day at sea if it is rough weather; some are very ill in their cabins, and the most valiant ones have bouillon or a wing of chicken served on deck; for one could not brave with impunity the unwholesome emanations of the cabin. I can well tell you so, as I have taken the trip five times. Dinner over, and night at hand, one was obliged to resign one's self at last, and enter one's state-room, no matter what happened. In the little quadrangle allotted to one, and which contains two frames, or berths, a toilet commode, and some portmanteaus [large suitcases], when you happen to be two, you can hardly open or close the door; you must therefore manage to get up and dress, one after the other. Under the lower berth you must be careful to have a little chest containing the body-linen necessary for your journey.

Two strings are placed at the head and foot of each bed. It is here you will successively stow away your travelling-bag, your fruit, your opera-glass, the few books which will be your travelling companions, your blotting-case, your fancy work if you are a woman, your box of cigars if you are of the opposite sex. This installation completed, it will be necessary, to get to your bed in the upper berth, to be past master in gymnastics, as the stool upon which you must step in order to get there is being swung from right to left by the rolling. Still, after many attempts, you seize a good moment and dart upwards, and there you are, finally resting between two boards which break your ribs, and constantly throw your poor body about as if you were the ball in a tennis court. Directly in front of me was an aperture by which I could distinguish the high waves encircling the ship on all sides, and a bit of sky where dark clouds were running. I felt so small before this grand ocean, so isolated in the midst of this sky and this sea, so "uncomfortably" installed, as our neighbors of the British Channel would say, that I would at any price have escaped from reality by sleep. Furthermore, did I draw it towards my assistance with all my being, and already was I beginning to feel its first drowsiness, when fresh hiccoughs were soon heard in the cabin adjoining ours, with the imploring cry, "Steward, a glass of sugar-water! Cabin-boy, the wash-bowl!" which was repeated with every shock of the waves.

A little peace finally succeeded all this tumult. Ten o'clock had just struck. All was hushed. The steward had completed the making-up of his bed on one of the settees in the cabin. Well, finally we would be able to sleep, I thought. Vain hope! Suddenly a child uttered piercing cries, and another, our *vis-à-vis*,* replied by the same method. Then my own child joined the party.

"What is the matter, my darling?"

*The person in the facing cabin—Ed.

"I have hurt myself."

"Drink a little water."

"No; I don't want to stay in a bed which moves. I want to sleep in my own little bed, which don't move."

"Poor darling! Put your little arms around my neck."

"Mamma, I feel sick."

Farther on was a consumptive, who was groaning and coughing; then the steward, tired of his day's work, was snoring at a terrible rate, and always, as an accompaniment to this tumult, the dull murmur of the waves beating against the sides of the vessel, the cracking of the timbers which seemed ready to burst asunder, the rolling which was shaking us incessantly, the dishes which were dancing in the pantry, and the wind which was blowing boisterously through the sails; then at different times the noise of the manœuvre and the monotonous singing of the sailors.

All this, I can assure you, may give the unhappy passenger of a first night on board some foretaste of the infernal regions [Hell].

Happily, towards three o'clock in the morning, succumbing to fatigue, we became unconscious of all; a heavy sleep was to restore our exhausted forces. Ah, well, yes! four o'clock strikes; immediately commences over our head the most horrible of mock serenades. A scraping, a brushing, a kicking begins, dull knocks awaken us by starts. Not knowing the meaning of all this noise, we hastened to go on deck, half dressed; but hardly have we risked it than we receive a large bucket of water over our feet, which gives us the key to all this bustle. All the sailors, legs and feet bare, are scrubbing the deck and quarter-deck; and I can assure you that neither hands nor buckets of water are spared.

Hoping to resume our interrupted sleep, we regained, however, what was called our bed. But below the same racket soon begins. The steward, assisted by the cabin-boy, washes and cleans the cabin. When he has put everything in order, replaced the racks upon the table, polished the brasses, and that everything glistens to his heart's content, this king of the cabin gravely pulls a bell, signal for the first repast. It is seven o'clock.

At this call, one state-room after another opens, to let forth heads more or less ridiculous in their head-dresses of the night, some of whom even are decorated with the classic nightcap. The men group themselves around the table, taking coffee, tea, the majority liquor.

It is rare, even during the most beautiful days, that the women ever appear at this first breakfast: the steward serves them in their state-rooms. Everybody after this is busy with their dressing and surroundings; and when at ten o'clock the *real* breakfast hour rings, the doors reopen anew, to let pass this time carefully combed heads and freshly shaven chins.

Now is the moment when all will find themselves reunited for the first time, and know with whom they are travelling, for the evening before one had hardly caught a glimpse of their fellow-passengers. Each one looks at the other without recognition, yet with careful scrutiny.

Rest assured, then, that the lady placed at the captain's right is the one whom this one considers the most noted of his lady passengers, either from the stand-point of beauty, or money, or that of social position. The lady placed at his left would naturally succeed the other as having right to attentions and little thoughtfulnesses. After this, the other lady passengers place themselves as they choose or agree. However, generally the most distinguished ones occupy the centre of the table, and the others the foot.

Now, I think I must give you some advice, ladies: if ever you travel alone, be on board the most reserved possible; for there is no little provincial town, no janitor's closet even, where there is as much gossip as there. If you have, for travelling companions, English people, do not bow to them, above all, and do not even notice them the first eight days. The Englishman wishes to know whom he bows to, and gives himself the trouble of studying a little his people before risking the least politeness. Do you think he is very much in the wrong? But from the moment he has judged you worthy of his society, the Englishman becomes the most amiable travelling companion, obliging without being gallant, polished without flattery, and always a perfect gentleman in his relations with women.

Unfortunately, it is not always so with our own compatriots while travelling, who, in the majority, do not always show themselves very proper, presently showing gallantry, bordering upon silliness, to young and pretty women; by and by, rudeness, well-nigh vulgarity, towards old or ugly women; they do not know whether to compromise a woman, or turn her into ridicule. Mistrust, above all things, ladies, the officers on deck. Nothing equals the conceitedness of these gentlemen; they must at each passage inscribe a fresh conquest on their list. As the attentions, the welfare, the thousand details of material existence, depend upon them in some way or other, there are no end of provocations and flirtations which the lady passengers permit in their favor.

When, during one of these long voyages, there are on board one or two ladies,—how shall we say?—frivolous? yes,—well then, it is a race between them which one shall carry it off, by captivating the captain, the first officer, the purser. In reality, to be in the captain's good graces means to have the best place, the best cut, to have the tent spread on the after-deck on calm and sunny days, to have a comfortable easy-chair, to be authorized to keep light in one's state-room; it is to obtain permission to have one's trunks carried up at any time from between-decks, so as to be able to exhibit each day a fresh toilet; it is, in short and above all, to surpass all the other women. Judge of the efforts! the many killing glances to get there!

There are generally on board three or four kinds of lady travellers, whom I have met with in all my travels. The first one is she whom I would call the *poseuse*. That one, on account of her rank or fortune, thinks herself *so* much above her fellow-travellers that she but rarely deigns to appear at table. Ordinarily, she is served in her state-room, occupies alone the best room, does not deign to exchange a few words but with the captain, has an air of not even seeing the other people, passes two or three hours at her toilet, and does not put in an appearance until nearly two o'clock, always accompanied by her lady's-maid, carrying her cloak or her vinaigrette.*

The second one belongs to a certain class called—well, never mind. That one dresses two or three times a day, laughs and speaks very loud; is generally on the best of terms with the first officer and the purser, takes one day the airs of an *ingénue*, and the next day says things which would make a dragoon blush; passes her days stretched at full length on the settees on deck, with her hair to the wind, without losing an occasion of showing foot and limb; makes it uncomfortable for other women; sings operatic airs when night approaches; dances and waltzes Thursdays and Sundays; remains on deck until one o'clock in the morning with the officers and gentlemen of her choice; and defrays the voyage by a lot of episodes more or less piquant.

The third one of these lady travellers is the "earnest" one, or the "*artiste*," speaking with all, without becoming intimate with any; going on deck, when every one leaves it, to enjoy a beautiful sunrise or a fine moonlight; arranging her day so as to keep a few hours for study or solitude, attending to her correspondence, reading, embroidering; dressed simply, but gloved with care, and having well-fitting boots; never joining in gossip, neither seeking nor escaping the society of her fellow-travellers; not desiring to carry off any one's heart, remaining calm amidst all these littlenesses and all these

*A small decorative bottle with a perforated top that holds smelling salts or aromatic vinegar—Ed.

vanities, incurring the respect of all, and frequently more surrounded at the end of the voyage than those who have tried to
be so. It is in this class, ladies, that we advise you to place yourself if you ever happen to travel alone, which, we trust, you
may not.

From the second day of the voyage, every one has already
their likes and dislikes. One exchanges a few bows, even a few
conventionalities. The third day conversations are begun.

There is the communicative passenger, who only asks to
disclose his heart to you, and tells you all his family histories;
he neither spares you a cousin nor an aunt, and interrupts,
from time to time, to go and get a photograph of his father,
mother, sisters, brothers, and cousins. You absolutely must
know even about the nurse of his nephew.

Then comes the melancholy passenger, a handsome youth,
who poses as "disappointed in love," while sending languishing glances to the ladies whom he softens, and who, all of them,
would already console him. He exhibits, also, on certain days,
the picture of the hard-hearted one, which he keeps night and
day upon his heart. That one has all the chances to be adored,
for obstacle is a strong attraction, and each daughter of Eve
dreams in secret to cure this poor lover of his unhappy
passion.

After this, we have the *stirring-up* passenger, always having a refrain on his lips, his mustache turned upwards, his trousers *à la hussarde*,* treating the officers nearly every day to
champagne, and paying court to the "free and easy one," and
to the lady's-maid of the *poseuse*.

Finally, the disagreeable passenger, always dissatisfied with
the food, the steamer's progress, the manners of the officers,
the bearing of the ladies, the weather, which he presently finds
too hot, and by and by too cold. He speaks at low voice in a
corner, like a conspirator, and tries to recruit around him all

*Like a hussar; that is, in a military style—Ed.

the disagreeables of the steamer. He is generally the one whom one sees appearing in the morning in the classic head-gear of a cotton bonnet or nightcap; souvenir of his former trade, probably. At the end of eight days, one knows the tastes and habits of each one. There is still, from time to time, some little event which breaks the monotony of every day,—a gold-headed, doree* has been caught, a shark is being harpooned, a cloud is in the sky; those are the islands of the Green cape,† which one sees, then the Azores; then some ship is hailed; but all this does not prevent time from hanging heavily on those especially who do not know how to employ themselves on sea as well as land. It is when arriving in this region, called by the sailors the *Pot au noir* [the Doldrums], situated nearly under the equator, that the deck's physiognomy takes a strange aspect. Imagine, reader, an oppressive, heavy heat, debilitating and over exciting all at once, where not a breath comes to spread the sails; the water of the sea resembles oil; the least bit of sleep is only gained by leaving skylights open, and finally even the cabin doors are left open, for this loss of air from which one suffers so much; one awakes at night with one's hair drenched in perspiration; the women can only wear muslin wrappers; the men, white trousers and coats; all drag themselves about, hardly speaking; looks are languishing, and gallant adventures are the order of the day; billets-doux are exchanged, and a day does not pass that has not its little scandal and its attack of nerves. What do you wish? It is nobody's fault, apparently. This exciting temperature crazes one at such a point that at night I have often thought myself under the power of *hashish*, so much my mind was floating while waking and sleeping, taking alternately dream for reality, and reality for dream. It is there that the old women with the young hearts have chances of success. All men acknowledge it: in the *Pot au*

---

*Doré, the walleyed pike—Ed.
†Cape Verde Islands—Ed.

noir women no longer have age, and those which were thought dreadful at the beginning of the voyage become suddenly charming, declarations abound, the defeats are numerous. Poor husbands, who allow your wives to travel alone, mistrust yourselves of the *Pot au noir*. Finally, after five or six days passed in this suffocating region, we arrive in the equator. Here will be baptized those who have not before passed it. The day of the passage of the line is still more crazy than the rest. I had read that the sailors disguised themselves, and that one of them played the role of the "Fathers" of the strait. That may be, but I have not seen it; and I will never tell you anything that I have not *seen*, wishing that these notes on Brazil, in default of other merit, have at least that one of perfect veracity.

I will therefore say, that when I passed for the first time on board a sailing ship I saw, the first thing in the morning, the young officers pursue with pails of water the passengers whose age would permit this fooling and baptize them by will or force, in leading even the reluctant ones under the pump (which, in these latitudes, has no difficulties). I also was prepared to be baptized, for there were among our passengers three creatures with whom I avoided speaking and whom I had often heard whisper when I passed them, "Haughty prude!" and other petty sayings of this kind. I was therefore convinced that they would profit of the occasion that day to receive me with some good bucketfuls of water. There was nothing of the sort. I was nursing at this time my eldest son, as I have said previously. The women respected in me the mother and the nurse. I was touched by this delicacy, which I certainly did not suspect in them, and not less touched in the evening, when the boatswain, who had composed for the occasion some verses where each passenger had his little hit, said, when coming to him, which was in running verse, which I do not remember: "Hush! there is a mother who is rocking her child to sleep; let us pass noiselessly, leaving the child sleep upon his mother's heart."

The day was passed in shouts of laughter and chasing over the bridge or deck; the sailors had double rations, and danced in the evening, having as music the singing of their comrades and the roaring of the waves. Those who have not passed a night on the ocean, softly raised by the waves, lighted by a splendid moon, and lulled by the songs of the sailors, cannot get an idea of what is most grand and most poetic in the world. When, later, I have again found myself in a ball-room or theatre, and I have heard each one around me say, "Oh, how beautiful! how fairy-like!" I have called up in my mind the souvenir of a night on board; I have seen again the vessel with its spreading sails cutting the waves, sinking softly to rise proudly, in leaving behind her a headway of light; I have seen again the pilot at the helm, the passengers picturesquely grouped on deck, and fantastically illuminated by that silvered light of the moon which poetizes everything, the night-watch walking the deck with measured step, and the sailors at the head of the ship, in the rigging, on the mizzen-mast, singing in chorus the refrain which they love, "Toward the shores of France, sailing in singing, sailing softly!" having always for an obliging accompaniment the murmuring billows and the slight crackling of the clipper cutting the waves. The immense ocean then seemed again new to me, blending with the sky at the horizon; I seemed again to feel blowing over my face that fresh breeze of the ocean, impregnated with its perfume, and, casting my eyes about me, involuntarily compared these shows of men with the magnificent spectacle of nature. How little, miserable, and prosaic all this seemed to me near the grand works of God! No, I repeat it, no one who has not seen the grand ocean scenes can understand the sublime and lasting impressions they create. The soul receives an ineffaceable impression, and seems reaching towards eternity before the vast horizons.

After this enthusiastic digression, which I hope my readers will pardon, I resume my narrative.

If the passage is good, one arrives at Rio Janeiro, by a clipper, in twenty-nine or thirty days, and in twenty days by a steamer; but when the wind is contrary, quite frequently it takes even forty days.

Two days before the arrival we had perceived land. What great joy for all to see again trees and vegetation, after so long a time passed between sky and water! Everybody was on deck; one no longer sleeps, one no longer eats any more.

At last, here is Brazil, which appears with its bouquets of banana-trees and palm-trees. One begins to distinguish the chain of mountains called the Giant, which represents well enough in effect a man of colossal stature stretched at full length, and whose profile resembles that of Louis XVI. That one which is called the Pão d'assucar [de açúcar] (Sugar-loaf)

Sugar Loaf   Church "da Gloria"

is the mountain which forms the foot of the Giant. It lies at the entrance of the bay of Rio Janeiro. Soon the ship enters the port, having at its right the fortress of Santa Cruz, and at its left the fortress of Sage [Lage], where it is hailed as it passes;

if it delays in stopping, a cannon-shot warns it not to continue its route. It then hoists its flag. "Where does she come from?" is asked. "How many days at sea?" "What is her name and that of her captain?" "Are there any ill on board?" After having satisfactorily answered all these questions, she enters the bay and throws anchor near a fort called Villa-Gaghâo [Villegaignon]. Immediately two little boats approach her; the one is the *alfândega* (custom-house boat), the other *sande* [*saude*] (health boat). The first one takes charge of the baggage and verifies the passports of the passengers; the second one, which has on board one of the principal physicians of the marine, who takes information as regards the sanitary conditions, and whether it is not necessary to quarantine the ship's crew. During this time, arrive from all sides different shore-boats, of which the largest are called *falûas*, and which take passengers with a part of their luggage. The heavy baggage is sent to the custom-house, where it will not be delivered until the next day, after the inspection.

These *falûas*—a kind of large bark with a high lateen-sail—are generally run by five robust negroes; the boss sits at the helm, while the other four row lightly, in cadenza, rising on their seats with each stroke of the oar, reseating themselves to rise anew. This was one of my first surprises, that these blacks, naked to the waist, brutal and beastly faces, marked with large scars (when they are the Minas negroes), the perspiration running down their body, impassible as statues, look at you without curiosity or surprise, and do not seem to trouble themselves neither about you nor anything else in the world, excepting to eat or sleep. These strange faces impress themselves. While they are rowing us on shore, throw a glance with me over this splendid bay, bordered on all sides with mountains covered with the most luxuriant vegetation. This one—all crooked and pointed—is called the Corcovado (the Hunchback); we will allow a few pages for it later. Here is another square at the top,—which is named Tiguca [Tijuca]. The cascade it encloses is famous. It is one of the most beautiful sites in Rio Janeiro.

Finally, at your left, the mountain, from which you see the fine outlines detach themselves towards the blue sky, is the Serra dos Orgãos (Organ Mountain), because in effect its crests resemble the form of organs in a church. Charming islets are spread over the bay, the borders of which are filled with orange-trees, cotton-trees, and banana-trees, always green and laden with fruit; the *chácaras* (villas) are situated in the midst of these bouquets of trees, and on an elevation at your left rises the little church of da Gloria, under the invocation of Nossa-Senhora da Gloria. At the right of the bay is the island das Cobras (of Serpents), then San [São] Domingo, and Praia-Grande, the ancient capital of Brazil. A pure sky of a most superb blue above your head, a warm sun gilding the landscape, king-fishers diving about you and flying off with a sudden flap of the wings with a fish in their beak, the sea blue and calm as a lake, a little breeze which comes to refresh you from far and wide,—this is what plunges you upon your arrival in a sort of beatitude and ecstasy; you remain literally dazzled.

Well, at last the *falûa* lands: now we have arrived. The negroes step into the water and carry me off in their strong arms to land me on terra-firma, for the borders of the bay are but an infected basin of refuse of all kinds, decaying, and distributing the most nauseating emanations. This was our first disillusion. These shores, which from a distance seemed so beautiful and so perfumed, were the receptacles of the city's filth and rubbish. Since then sewers have been made. We landed at *Farû* wharf, *largo do paco* [paço] (place of the palace).

The Emperor's palace was the first edifice which met our gaze. There is little about it to excite admiration. It is a large, square building, which, in landing, I took for barracks. In front of the palace is the market, which is really one of the most picturesque parts of the city. There the large Minas negresses, with their head-dress in the shape of a muslin turban, their faces full of scars and seams, having a chemise and a skirt with ruffles as their clothing, are squatted on mats, near their fruits

My Negress "Romana"

or vegetables; at their sides are their boys and girls, in complete nudity.

Those whose children are still at the breast carry them fastened to their backs with a large piece of striped cloth, which then is passed two or three times around their bodies, after having first placed the child on their hips, feet and arms straddled. The poor little thing remains thus all day, shaken about by the movements of its mother, with its nose cushioned on her back when it sleeps, and having no holding-place, but rolling constantly from right to left; its little limbs are so straddled by the violent stoop of the negress that many become bow-legged.

Nothing [is] more original than the aspect of this market, where are piled up oranges, bananas, mangoes, Conda [*Conde*] fruits [sweetsop], watermelons, pineapples, lemons, Indian pears, pomegranates, *espinafres, palmitoes* [*palmito*], *batatas doces,** in the midst of parrots of all kinds, of *tatus* [armadilloes], of monkeys, turkey-hens, and birds of all feathers or plumage.

Farther on are found the sellers of mats, cocoas, gourds, and large jars, the smallest of which, called *moringas*, are the decanters of the country.

At the end, looking towards the sea, is found the fish market, where abound sardines, shrimps, oysters, and delicious

*Spinach, hearts of palm, sweet potatoes—Ed.

fishes, which are bought alive. All along the wharf, which borders the market on this side, are the canoes, or *canœs* [*canoas*]
where the fishermen sell the fish in lots. There stand, under
large linen umbrellas, negresses, who serve you, for two cents,
a bowl of hot coffee, or else some smoking *batatas doces*, fried
sardines, and some *angú* (manioca flour mixed with boiling
water and salt, and forming a sort of thick *bouillon*). The
negroes, who are most dainty, even season everything with a
sort of fat they call *azeite de dindin* (*dindin* [dendê]* oil). There,
also, are sold the *massarocas* [*massarocos*] of Indian wheat broiled,
and the *feijöada* [*feijoada*]†,—that is to say, all that constitutes,
in Brazil, a negro's repast, and even that of the white people of
the inferior classes. It is there that one must hear spoken that
African language, which is called the coast language. Nothing
[is] more strange; it seems as if no consonant entered. One can

Imperial Chapel and "Carmos" Church

*An oil extracted from the fruit of the African oil palm—Ed.
†A dish made up of black beans cooked with pieces of various meats—
Ed.

absolutely distinguish nothing but some "*ohui, ya ahua, o, y, o.*"
I had learned a few words, which I have quickly forgotten. It is
almost impossible to retain a language of which one completely
ignores the orthography.

Part II
Rio Janeiro

*W*hen you enter the city of Rio Janeiro by the *largo do paço*, the first street which presents itself to you is Dircita [Direita] Street (right). It is one of the most beautiful streets of the city; it is quite wide, and bordered on each side by houses of one or two stories, painted in different colors, having, in the majority, their balconies decorated with red and white blinds. The majority of houses are of ancient construction; many even have kept the verandas around the residences. This street is very lively, for it is here the stock exchange* is held. Three or four beautiful churches, among others Santa Cruz and the church dos Carmos [do Carmo] (*see engraving*), are remarkable.

The whole length of the street, on the steps of the churches, or at the doors of the shops, are squatted the large Minas negresses (the Minas originally came from the province of Mina, in occidental Africa), adorned in their most beautiful things: a fine chemise, and a skirt of white muslin with ruffles, worn over another skirt of some bright color, form all their costume; they have their feet bare in a sort of slipper with high heel, called *tamancas* [*tamancos*], where only the point of the foot can enter; their neck and their arms are loaded with gold chains, strings of pearl, and all sorts of pieces of ivory and of teeth, sort of manitous,† which, according to them, must conjure evil fortune; a large piece of muslin is rolled three or four times around their head, turban shape, and another piece of

---

*Not a modern stock exchange but rather a trading center—Ed.
†Spirits, deities, or objects that possess supernatural power—Ed.

striped cloth is thrown over their shoulders, to cover themselves with when they are cold, or to encircle their hips when
they carry a child. (*See engraving.*)

Many men find these negresses handsome; as for me, I
acknowledge that the curled wool, which does duty for hair,
their low and debased forehead, their blood-shot eyes, their
enormous mouth with bestial lips, their disjointed teeth, like
those of deer, as well as their flattened nose, had never appeared to me to constitute but a very ugly type. What is the
least vulgar is their carriage. They walk with head held high,
chest prominent, hips raised, arms akimbo, holding their load
of fruits always placed on the head. Their feet and their hands
are small, their waists are firm and curving, and their walk of
easy gait, is always accompanied by a movement of the hips
quite suggestive, and yet filled with a certain dignity, like that
of the Spanish woman. Their bosom is hardly veiled by their
fine chemise, and sometimes even one breast is seen; but few
among them have fine necks. It is only in the very young
mulattresses that this beauty is sometimes found.

As regards the negresses nothing has been exaggerated in
saying that they easily nursed their children placed on their
backs. I have seen it done by some of my servants, only that it
is really not from the middle of the back that the child nurses,
but from under the arm. There is nothing more debauched
than these Minas negresses; they are the ones who deprave
and corrupt the young people of Rio Janeiro; it is not rare to
see foreigners, especially Englishmen, maintain them and ruin
themselves for them.

It is not rare either to hear of the *facadas* (knife-cuts) given
to the whites by the jealous blacks.

When one desires these creatures, one has only to make
them a sign, and they follow one. I have had some in my house,
who, their work being finished, would disappear to give themselves up to this fine trade, and found it very singular I should
reprimand them on the subject. They'd reply very simply, "I

must go and earn something with which to buy a piece of lace. Our Brazilian ladies are not like madam, and allow us several hours each evening for that."

My intention not being to give the nomenclature of the streets of Rio Janeiro and its monuments, I will leave the subject, after having said a word, however, on the street do Ouvidor, essentially a French street, where the stores of our modistes [milliners], of our hair-dressers, of our florists, and of our pastry-cooks are displayed in all their splendor. It is the daily rendezvous of the "young men about town," who, under the pretext of buying some cigars or cravats, come to flirt with the Frenchwomen, on whom they dote. This street, although narrow and ugly, is in some sort the *Boulevard des Italiens** of the capital of Brazil. One hears only French spoken,—and what a kind of French! My goodness! It is there that the importance of our compatriots who left home as workmen, and who since have become proprietors of stores, is ridiculous to see,—so proud to have money and slaves, they hardly deign to honor you with a pat-on-the-back bow.

I was received on my arrival at an ex-plumber's and his wife's,—*parvenus* in the full strength of the term,—in a manner that was most amusing. The husband, a large man, wearing ear-rings, could not speak a word without accompanying it with a mistake, and did not open his mouth but to speak of his dollars and his slaves. As to his wife,—very important, too, as she called herself,—spreading herself out in her arm-chair in *décolleté* [low-cut] dress, which showed that which she should have hidden with care, interrupting at every instant her party in playing cards to call out: "O *négrinha*" (little negress), "pass me my fan!" "Oh, give me my snuff-box!" "O *négrinha*, bring me a glass of water!" "Oh, pick up my handkerchief!" and that handkerchief, above everything, she would throw down more than twenty times during the evening, so as to give herself the

---

*In Paris, then known for its dandies and café society—Ed.

pleasure of having it picked up as many times by a little negress of seven or eight years, squatted at her feet.

When they returned to France, they brought with them a little negro hardly five years old. It was a curiosity which they exhibited. I still can see that poor little unfortunate squatting in the corner of the mantel-piece, shivering in all his limbs; to warm him up, his masters would make him drink a glassful of brandy. At the end of six months, with these intelligent attentions, he died, without ever having been able to get warmed up.

This establishment had for friends an old clothes-dyer and a retired pastry-cook, who came to pass the evening two or three times a week; and I had the good fortune of happening in on one of those evenings. The French which I heard spoken in that reunion by those four people will never leave my memory. As they had, during their twenty or thirty years' sojourn in Brazil, about unlearned the little French they had ever known, and knowing still less the language of the country they had inhabited for so many years, they spoke an impossible idiom, insensible mixture of two tongues enamelled with such strange phrases that I thought I heard Chinese or Hebrew, and never could be persuaded that there really were four French people speaking to each other. You can imagine I never went again, although the ex-plumber's wife said, in putting one hand on her hip, and with the other fanning herself at full breeze, "I hope you have dined prettily, haven't you?" and that the husband at general request had tuned up to a song, of which each verse ended invariably by the refrain, which was sung in chorus, of, "And by preference I am a scavenger."

Hardly had we arrived at Rio Janeiro when we were asked from everywhere,—"Have you seen the Corcovado?" "When will you go to see the Corcovado?"

We therefore must go and see the Corcovado, and so a day was taken for the famous ascension.

Carioca Aqueduct

We started at three o'clock in the morning, for one must avoid as much as possible the heat of the day. Ordinarily, fifteen or twenty people meet to make a party. Our little caravan was composed of sixteen persons, without counting the darkies who followed us, carrying on their heads the large *cestos* (large bamboo baskets) containing provisions. As for the negresses, they had the care of the children, who are permitted to be of all parties, and who are even taken to the theatre, so much confidence is put in the slaves to take care of them. Sometimes mules are taken for the children and the provisions, and half of the mountain is ascended on horseback or donkey-back. The second time that I made the excursion to the Corcovado I made it in the latter way, and I acknowledge that I preferred it. One begins the ascension by Santa Thereza Mountain; halfway up you find the convent of women which bears this name, and which only will give shelter to one-and-twenty women. Turn around, then, and admire! At your feet stretches off the beautiful bay of Rio Janeiro, with its houses of all nations, with its mountains so beautifully curved, with its green islets which seem like opening bouquets in the sea.

I have often told myself that if ever the idea of becoming a nun had come to me, it could only have been at the convent of Santa Thereza that I should have come to ask for peace and meditation.

Before this grand nature our so-called civilized society pales indeed. There all human things disappear, and one can only think of God.

Ascending, still ascending. At your right the aqueduct, which, from the summit of the Corcovado, descends into the city to distribute this so famous water of the Carioca, which has given place to this Brazilian proverb, "Who has drunk of the waters of Carioca can drink no other water"; and to this other one, "You have drunk of the waters of Carioca: you can live nowhere else but here."

The inhabitants of Rio Janeiro have also the habit of saying of one of their compatriots who has lived in Rio, "He is a Cariocan."

Let us still ascend. Here the large trees are beginning to appear: to begin with, the mango-tree, with its bushy foliage, the tamarind-tree, the bread-tree; then on the plateaus, the banana-tree, with its substantial and savory fruit; the cocoa-tree, the orange-tree, which tosses over you its perfumed attire; the coffee-tree, with its little red seeds, and leaves of a dark and lustrous green; the palm-tree, of such picturesque effect in the Brazilian landscape; the lemon-trees, the cotton-trees,—what not? All this crosses, entwines, entangles itself, and forms over your head a dome of verdure, where the hottest rays of the sun cannot penetrate.

The fruits, the flowers, the grass, all invite you. But nature is perfidious here: beware! Poison is concealed under the most beautiful flowers and under the most savorous fruits; some serpent, perhaps, with its deadly venom, crawls under this beautiful turf which had its color; a scorpion is there waiting to give you a wound which you will not forgive. Remember that you are in Brazil, and beware, foreigners, and climb higher! At last we arrive at a place called Os Dous Irnâos [Irmãos] (the two brothers), on account of two triangular stones which are believed to go back to Dom Juâo [João] VI. Here our caravan halts. We choose a spot near the stream, on a fine eminence, which is explored with care, in the fear of objectionable company being found. The negroes filled the *canecas* (tin cans) with pure and sparkling water, of which Europeans can have no idea; the cloth was spread on a mat which answered for a table, and the whole company then commenced a frugal and charming repast, seasoned with much appetite.

The darkies formed a group apart, which was not the least of the tableau.

They had soon lit a fire with some small branches, and over two stones placed their pot, in which were being warmed *feijâoes* [*feijões* or black beans] (black peas), which they sprinkled with manioca flour; then kneading it all in their hands, and forming large balls, they commenced to throw them in their mouth with much dexterity. If you wish them to eat with a spoon, they all insist that it takes away much of the flavor of their *feijoada*.

During the breakfast, the *mucamas* (housemaids) fan away over our heads, with large banana leaves, the flies and mosquitoes.

The repast over, the climbing again begins, more laborious this time, for the sun was already hot, and we began to feel fatigued. The trees become more and more dense, the convolvulus[†] entwine them, and creeping plants of all kinds are suspended. Finally, we arrived at the *mai de agua* (the mother source).

*Trailing plants with trumpet-shaped flowers—Ed.

There the European can get an idea of those beautiful virgin forests which have not been undermined by our pitiless civilization. All human sound has ceased, only a rustling without name can be heard, dominated from time to time by the sharp whir of the grasshopper; there each blade of grass is inhabited; each tree, each leaf, contains a world; you see yourself alone, and yet you feel a multitude of beings stirring around you; hardly can one see the top of the century-old trees that surround one; it is an inextricable and grand chaos which seizes you; and I was lost in ecstasy before this wild and gigantic nature which inspired me all at once with terror and admiration.

Leaving aside the *mai de agua*, one must climb narrow, perpendicular paths, scarcely traced, and finally, after five or six hours' walking, one arrives on the summit of the Corcovado. The most beautiful panorama then unrolls itself before your eyes.

Still, I will admit that I was seized with more enthusiasm at the middle of the mountain than at its summit. I had imagined a little to myself the splendid view which would await me at such a height, but I had not foreseen the profound emotion I should feel at the aspect of nature coming virgin-like from God's hands.

We had been staying since our arrival at Rio Janeiro at our uncle's; but we wished to settle down by ourselves. After having travelled all over the city, we could not find what we wished but in Rosario Street. Alas! what a street for Parisians accustomed to all the comfort and all the luxury of our capital! The street is narrow, dull, and has for stores on the first floor of each house only *vendas*, that is to say, dull shops, where are piled up, mountain-like, the *carne secca* (dried meat), the *bacalhäo* (dried cod), the bags of *feijoes* and of rice, as well as the Minas cheeses.* When you arrive in this country you are far from imagining that this sort of leather rolled in bundles, which

*Cheese from the Province of Minas Gerais—Ed.

you see piled up in this way, can be meat. This is, however, the principal food of the country; and there is not a Brazilian who does not prefer the *carne secca* to the *carne verde* (green meat).* To tell you what a fearful odor emanates from this dried cod and meat is impossible: think that the street is narrow, never swept or sprinkled, that the sun of the tropics shines on it continuously, and try to give yourself an idea of the emanations which would arise therefrom!

It was there that my husband and I became ill with yellow fever, which dealt harshly with Brazil, for the first time, the year of our arrival. Until then the country had been very healthy. When this dreadful disease fell upon Rio Janeiro, it attacked first of all the foreigners, then the negroes, then the poor class, and finally the comfortable Brazilians themselves, but in small numbers.

The mortality was so large in the city, and the cemeteries so filled, that one could no longer bury the dead. No more festivals, no more disturbance, no more joy: everywhere mourning.

The theatres were closed; large processions passed through the city every day, praying to God for the end of the epidemic. At the head of the procession young girls walked dressed in white. When arriving at a public place, a bench would immediately be brought in the centre of the place, and upon this bench would step one of the young ladies, who would recite aloud the prayer, which all would say after her.

Nothing [was] more doleful than these litanies, sung monotonously and alone, breaking from time to time the dark silence which hovered over the city. Every morning we would hear of the death of some compatriot of ours. Of the twenty-eight passengers who had made the voyage with us, seventeen had already succumbed when I first began to feel this fever, of which I immediately recognized the symptoms.

*One might think green meant decayed; on the contrary, it means fresh.

A homœopathic physician had been recommended to us upon our arrival, called Dr. Paitre, and we had been presented to him. My husband went to him immediately, but it was useless: the doctor himself had been taken ill, and had quickly left the city, away from this hearth of contagion, in which it was so hard to arrive at recovery. What to do then? I drew out of my travelling-bag my case of homœopathic medicine, given by Hahnemann* himself before my departure, and searched for in the "Manuel de Jarl," which I had already studied, each of the symptoms of my illness. I began by administering to myself medicines, *veratrum* and *ipecacuanha* simultaneously. That same day the negress which we had hired also became ill, and we were obliged to send her back to her master. Then, after this, my husband's turn came, who suddenly felt himself taken with chills.

Hardly arrived here since three months, knowing no one in the city, scarcely seeing the relatives with whom we had at first been staying, without physician, without servant, with very little money, and a child of eighteen months, which I had just weaned,—such was our position. My husband had to take to his bed, and I was treating him as I was treating myself. Whoever felt best would get up to attend to the feeding of the child, who, fortunately, was not overtaken with it. I had the happiness of saving us both, and we entered into convalescence. I directed it, after my own fashion, with strong bouillon, where I would throw in a handful of cooked sorrel; then a little boiled beef and rice cooked in water would complete the repast. Thanks to this diet, of an excessive moderation, our stomachs became perfectly strong, and since, every time that the yellow fever has visited the country during the twelve years that we have inhabited it, we never again were attacked with it. It must be said that this sickness attacks with far more violence those who live in excesses, of whatever nature, it may be of drink, for

*Samuel Hahnemann (1755–1843), a German physician who was the founder of homeopathy—Ed.

example, or even fruits. Oranges eaten in quantities have led more than one new arrival to the tomb. The Brazilians never eat an orange that they pick from the tree; they pretend that in this way they give fever; they must be allowed to cool, as they say, before they can be good.

The yellow fever is now acclimatized in Brazil, as the cholera is in our countries. It appears from time to time in the great heat, but no longer shows itself so deadly as in the first year, because one knows how to treat it.

One must, in the tropical countries, observe more moderation than anywhere else. Those who, having the custom of wine and liquors, wish to continue in Brazil the same manner of living, don't do so for long.

Do as the natives do: drink water. Besides, the water is so good in Rio that this beverage is nearly a treat. Also, does the Brazilian drink his four or five glasses in an evening, it is so limpid, so perfumed, so light, this water of the Carioca, which winds through white pebbles, across aromatic plants, and comes to you fresh and full of odors, which one ever remembers, and which the Brazilian has a right to say, "When one has drunk that water, one can drink no other."

We had as a neighbor in Rosario Street, in the upper story, a Spanish señora, who had at her service three or four slaves. Every day the most terrible scenes took place over our head. For the least omission, for the least fault of either of them, the señora would beat them or give them blows with the *palmatoria* (a sort of little palette pierced with holes), and we would hear these poor negresses throw themselves on their knees, in crying, "Mercy! señora!" But the pitiless mistress would never be touched, and gave without pity the number of blows she would consider necessary to be given. These scenes would give me great pain.

One day, when the blows of the *chicote* (whip) rained harder than ever, and when the screams were heard more heart-rending than usual, I arose all at once, and addressing myself to my husband, who, born in Brazil, of French parents, spoke Portuguese as his native language,—"How do you say executioner?" I asked him.

"*Carasco [carrasco]*," he replied, without understanding why I set him this question. Immediately I rush to the stairs, which I mount in running. I open the door of the señora, flinging this one word at her, "*Carasco!*" This was my first word of Portuguese. That woman remained stupefied. Afterwards, hearing no noise whatever, I thought I had saved these unfortunate ones. Nothing of the kind: simply since that time she gagged them, so that their screams should no longer reach me. This was all that they had gained. This sight of slavery was, during the first years of my sojourn in Brazil, one of the torments of my life, and did not in a little contribute to give me homesickness, of which I expected to die. At every instant my heart revolted or bled when I passed before one of those *leitãos [leilões]* (auctions), where the poor negroes, standing upon a table, were put up at auction, and examined by their teeth and their legs, like horses or mules; when I saw the auction over, and that a young negress was being handed over to the *fazendeiro* [plantation owner], who would reserve her for his "intimate" service, while her little child was sometimes sold to another master. Before all these scenes of barbarism my heart would rise up and generous anger would boil in me, and I was obliged to do me violence in not screaming to all these men who were making a traffic in human flesh, "*Carascos!*" as I had flung it at my Spanish neighbor. Scarcely had I succeeded in pacifying myself, than I would meet a few steps farther a poor negro wearing a mask of iron. This was still the fashion in which drunkenness was punished on the slave some twelve or fifteen years ago. Those who drank were condemned to wear a mask of iron, which was on the back of the head by means of a chain, and which was only removed during meals. One cannot imagine the impression caused by these men with iron heads. It was frightful; and think what a torment under this heat of the tropics! Those who had run away were fastened by one leg to a post; others carried around their neck a large iron collar, a kind of yoke, like that which is put upon oxen; others, in short, were sent to the *correccâo* [*casa de correcão*] (penitentiary), where, after they had been bound to a post, they would be lashed forty, fifty, or even sixty times. When the blood would flow they would stop, their wounds would be dressed with vinegar, and the day following it would begin again. One must not accuse the Emperor of Brazil for this state of things. He is, on the contrary, full of kindness, and his slaves are treated with great mildness; but he had found these customs established in mounting upon the throne, and could not modify in a day these customs of the country; he had to close his eyes on the slave-trade, for they alone were able to bear the labors of tillage under this burning sun.

One had endeavored to bring colonists from all countries, so as to gradually substitute them for negroes: but the French scarcely resisted a few months; the English, who wished to continue their gin-system, would soon die of its effects; the Chinese, lazy and impoverished race, would not give any good result; the Germans alone had been able to found a little colony; besides it was in the high and mountainous regions of the country, where the climate a little approaches that of Europe. What to do then? If slavery were suddenly abolished, the country would be ruined. The Emperor found himself before all these difficulties.

The only race fit for farming in Brazil is, without question, the native race, *os Indios, os Caboclos (see engraving)*, as the Brazilians call them. But, hunted down as it has been, refusing to submit, taking refuge in the depth of the forests, wild, flesh-eating even in some parts, one does not expect to be able to subjugate it so soon. As to the Brazilian race, a mixture of European, American, and African blood, it has all the creole indolence, is weak, corrupted, very intelligent, and not less arrogant. It is evident that it is to the intercourse with the

Caboclos

negroes that is due, in a measure, the impoverishment of this race. The negresses, with their African ardors, demoralize the young people of Rio Janeiro and her provinces.

There is in their blood a bitter principle which kills the white man. The negro's tooth even is frequently dangerous. I have seen more than one example, in Brazil, of European overseers (for never does a Brazilian himself strike his slave), who, in beating their negroes, had been bitten by them, or even only had been touched by their teeth, who were obliged to have their arm amputated.

The Brazilian race could not stand hard labor; besides, it despises all manual labor. Not a Brazilian would consent to be employed; all wish to be proprietors. If, therefore, slavery had been suddenly abolished, farming would have stopped, and famine would have arisen. One had to gradually prepare the country and the minds for this grand revolution. This was what Dom Pedro II did; and when, according to him, the hour had come, he declared free each slave's son who would be born in the future.* In this way, the negroes, happy to know their children free, bear their bondage with more courage; and when

---

*The Law of the Womb, or Rio Branco Law, passed in 1871, emancipated all children of slave mothers born after the legislation went into effect. But under its complicated provisions, those children could be obliged to labor for their masters until the age of twenty-one if their masters had chosen that option rather than the option of taking care of them until the age of eight and then receiving an indemnification from the state—Ed.

their sons will come to earn their living in the country which has given them birth, it is likely they will remain and till the ground for them, in short.

Only the large number of free negroes is a great black spot in the Brazilian horizon; their number already surpasses that of the whites. It might be feared, perhaps, that when they should have counted their numbers, they might be taken by terrible revenge, and that the future would avenge the past. Let us hope, however, that Brazil will not have its San Domingo.*

That which is most appalling is the mulatto race. It is evident that this is the race which will be called some day to govern the country. It is said to have the virtues and defects of the two races from which it springs, and gives proof of a remarkable intelligence. It is already among the mulattoes that are counted the most celebrated physicians of Rio, as also her most remarkable statesmen.

But let us return to my travelling impressions. Among the things whose oddity struck me most upon my arrival I must speak of the processions. I was invited by a French merchant to come and see, to begin with, the passing of the Maundy Thursday procession, which is called that of the *Corpo de Dêos*, and later on, that of the *San Jorge*. All the windows in town on those days were adorned with curtains of red, blue, or yellow damask, and at every window the Brazilian ladies showed themselves off in full dress; that is to say, in a black silk dress, *décolleté*, the neck and ears loaded with diamonds. Beside them were their children, surrounded by little mulattoes and negroes, and behind stood the *amas seccas*, or nurses.

The Holy Thursday procession does not start until night. *Sâo José* and *Nossa Senhora* begin the procession, carried each

---

*The only completely successful slave revolt in the New World occurred in the 1790s in Saint Domingue, the western third of the island of Hispaniola —a long, bloody, devastating struggle against the French that gave rise to the first independent nation in Latin America, Haiti—Ed.

by six mulattoes or negroes; then comes Jesus Christ on the cross between the two thieves; and finally, Judas, who the following day must be burned in effigy in the form of a straw manikin in all parts of the city.

Before and behind these saints walk the angels; that is to say, little girls of five or six years of age, wearing very short skirts, all embroidered in gold, and as full and puffed as the hoop-skirts of our grandmothers. Two large wings of gauze are fastened on their back, and they have on their head a diadem of jewels. They must march, in leaping, to a harmonious rhythm, and take leave in strewing on their way rose-leaves contained in a little basket which they hold in their hand. On both sides, forming the line, file off one by one the Brazilians, the mulattoes, and even the free negroes, wearing each the dress of the secular brotherhood to which they belong; that is to say, a sort of cape or hood of red, blue, or yellow silk, according to the *irmandade* (order), and having all in their hand a long burning taper. The Emperor and Empress always follow the Holy Thursday procession. They stop at seven churches, in remembrance of the seven stations of Christ.

The procession of St. George is more curious still, on account of the manikin who represents the saint. It is a manikin all barbed with iron, carrying a helmet, whose visor is lowered; he is perched on a lean horse, and at his sides walk two equerries, whose sole occupation is to restore St. George's equilibrium in his saddle. Nothing [is] more grotesque than to see this manikin with each start of the horse bending presently to the right, presently to the left, or suddenly flattening his nose against the mane of his horse. One would not dare laugh. One should see with what respect the two equerries replace the great saint to his equilibrium, and how every one prostrates themselves before him during his passing. These procession days are the great festivals of the country, as also St. John's Day, when the Brazilian families have the custom of receiving, and inviting each other to a *tomar huma chicara de châ* or *beber um copo de agua* (take a cup of tea or drink a glass of water); it is the consecrated formula to invite you to a *soirée*, a dance, the most frequently.

[On] St. John's Day large fires are lit on all the public places of the city, and in these *fogueiras* are roasted *batatas doces* and sugar-cane, which are served hot, on large trays, towards the middle of the evening.

All these customs are beginning to vanish at Rio Janeiro, but they are still observed religiously in the interior of the country. I have seen on these festival days some Brazilian ladies dance, by general request, the *lundû* (national dance), which the young women know nothing of at the present hour, and which consists of a kind of harmonious promenade, with a movement of the hips and eyes, which is not lacking in originality, and which ordinarily must be accompanied by everybody in snapping their fingers like castanets, so as to well keep the rhythm.

The man in this dance in some sort only turns around the lady and follows her, while she gives herself up to all kinds of the most bewitching cat-like movements.

The first time that I was invited at Rio to attend one of these balls, I remember while dancing that my eyes were carried towards the artist at the piano, and that I became very much impressed with the strange pallor overspreading his face. This pallor was so extraordinary that I could not refrain from asking if that gentleman, who might be thirty-five years old, was not very sick. I was told no, but that he had remained in this way since the day that he had killed his wife.

You may judge of the effect this reply gave me. I wished to know on the instant all the details of this tragic history, and here is what I was told: Mr. M——, one of our compatriots, had arrived three years ago with his wife, young and handsome, who had been engaged as a singer at the theatre of Rio. Bouquets and letters poured each evening at the feet of the charming artiste, and among the most passionate adorers was soon remarked a young physician of the town, who had made his studies in France, and whose mind had taken the sneering and sceptical turn proper to Parisians.

One day, seeing her ready to go out more dressed than usual, he had a suspicion that she was going to a rendezvous, and placing himself before her, said,—"You shall not go out!"

"I shall go out!" she replied, in moving toward the door.

Then the husband, drawing from his breast a pistol which he had concealed, levelled it at the young wife, and with two shots she fell lifeless at his feet. Then he gave himself up as prisoner. After having had judgment passed and [been] absolved by the law, he had remained in the country, where at each step he would meet the man who had dishonored him. He had had the sad courage of killing the woman, and had not that of killing the man.

All stained with his crime, carrying since, like an eternal stigma, that cadaverous pallor, he continued, however, to come and play each evening quadrilles and polkas for the dancing of the Brazilian youth, his crime having in some way made him fashionable. This story froze me; my eyes could not be taken from this man, who was generally pitied, while I could find no other word in looking at him but this only one, "Coward!" The ball soon lost for me, little by little, its joyful aspect; the black note was dominating, and I thought myself under sway of a Hoffmann tale,* and it seemed to me as if a vampire were leading the dance. I began to think of that young and beautiful creature, killed without pity in her prime, and I wished to know if the lover had at least kept her memory. I was told that at her death he had shown great grief.

---

*Ernst Theodor Amadeus Hoffmann (1776–1822), a German writer of fairy tales and ghost stories—Ed.

Part III
A Fazenda

———❦———

A change of air having been ordered me for a sort of slow fever of which I could not get rid, a Brazilian, whose acquaintance my husband had recently made, offered to take us to his *fazenda* and to stay a month, which we accepted most heartily, desirous as we were to visit a little the interior of the country, and to learn its customs.

The *fazenda*, as you doubtlessly know, is a plantation where particularly are cultivated rice, coffee, sugar-cane, *feijoes*, and manioca. There are some of these plantations which measure fifteen to twenty miles in length. The one to which we were invited was situated near a town called Mana, and was called the plantation of Sao Jozé [São José]. To get there we had to begin with crossing in a steamer the beautiful bay of Rio, strewn with charming islands, among which one remarks that of the Governador (governor), and the other, called Paquetá, which is charming with its luxuriant vegetation, and emerges out of the midst of the sea like an immense bouquet of flowers. It took us three hours to cross the bay in all its length, and I must say that the passengers which we had for travelling companions were not the fine flower of first blossoms. The ones, fat Portuguese *vendeiros* (grocers), would take off their shoes, and scratch their feet during the trip; the others were stretched on the settees, half dressed, and snoring, without trouble about their companions; some negroes, dirty and bad smelling, carrying baskets and merchandise of all kinds, encumbered the steamer, so that we were very well satisfied to leave this

51

charming society at Piedade. That was a sorry-looking port at that time. Only one habitation could be found,—a kind of large building whose immense sheds were used as warehouses for the city's merchandise, and also that of the interior. There stop all the _fazendeiros_, the _mascatos_ [_mascates_] (carriers), and the _tropeiros_ (mule-drivers).

To all these people rooms are let whose beds must be occupied, I assure you; food is also given. Under the _rancho_ are ranged, pell-mell, mules, horses, sheep, and pigs. It was there that our saddle-beasts had to await us. I was shown to a room, so that I could, at my ease, put on my riding-habit. The filth of this place cannot be described. Never, do I believe, had a broom visited it! I did not know where to lay the garments which I took off, neither those I was to put on; the chairs were covered with dust, and the beds were still more dirty; so that I turned around for more than a quarter of an hour before I could decide to dress. I had finally just gotten into my riding-habit when the Senhor P—— came to tell us that his page was awaiting us with our saddle-beasts. With that word "page," my thoughts immediately pictured a cherubim. I pictured to myself a young and fair boy in silken stockings and doublet of velvet. But, alas! instead of the ideal page, I beheld a blubber-lipped negro, with flat nose, sheep's wool for hair, and who had been dressed up in a large red livery, whose faded lace gave its history, and which had, without doubt, formerly figured at the Théâtre Français, and successively at all the other theatres in Paris before coming to ornament the shoulders of the poor African, who wore with it trousers of coarse linen, and enormous silver spurs, which were held by a leather strap over his ugly bare feet. Such was the page who awaited us. I was taken, when I beheld him, with a desire to laugh outrageously, which cost me much pain to suppress during my whole journey. Whenever my eyes would be cast over his garb, I would be reminded of the fantastical lucubrations [laborious studies] of Chicard. His master saluted him with these words: "_O senhor_ *patifo* [*patife*]!" (O stupid man!) "*O burro!*" (O donkey!) and this continued, in the same tone, during the whole time that he harnessed the horses.

Finally we started, I, on horseback, at the side of the *do illustrissimo senhor fazendeiro*; then my husband beside my eldest son, who was hardly seven, and yet held himself well in the saddle. The route in leaving Piedade is, to begin with, very unsightly, almost without vegetation for at least a few miles. The horses walk in sand, which seems to prove that the sea formerly covered this part of the country. Little by little trees appear, and finally one skirts the virgin forest, where the cries of the monkeys and parrots come to remind you that you are in Brazil.

We had to ascend every now and then little mountains with such narrow paths that, having met other riders, who crossed us, we were obliged, to allow them to pass, to stand our horses on the very wall of the rock, and another time, having found myself, on the contrary, on the outside of the precipice, I will acknowledge that I had a certain fear, for a single movement of my horse would have precipitated me into the ravine. After this the way becomes a delight. One sees only convolvulus and creeping plants encircling the large trees. It is a frame-work of leaves, flowers, fruits, more charming than all that man arranges, or, more correctly speaking, disarranges. I could not become tired of admiring it. We suffered a little by the heat; but in Brazil there is always a breath of air, which revives you. When the country breezes have finished blowing, the sea breezes begin in their turn. They are called in this country, the one the *terral*, and the other the *viração*. It is owing to these benevolent breezes that one becomes able to stand a heat of ninety degrees in the shade.

With what pleasure I recall my horseback rides, when the wind blew through my hair and sent me the perfume of magnolias and orange blossoms! I acknowledge that nature gave me grand pleasures in Brazil, and it was always with an immense

feeling of happiness that I found myself on horseback gallop-
ing in the midst of this wild country.

After three hours of travel, we had arrived at the *fazenda*
Sao Jozé. It was six o'clock in the evening, and the sun was
beginning to set. The cattle were returning from all parts, led
by the shepherds, and had grouped themselves near the stiles
which surrounded the habitation, waiting to have them opened.
To enter, we should be obliged to pass through *la boiada*, which
is to say, a herd of a hundred oxen, cows, and bulls, which were
in our way. At the sight of those threatening horns, I declared
to my host that I did not feel the courage to advance. He smilingly reassured me, and told me to follow him without fear.
Follow him I did, but without fear I would not affirm. All those
beasts vied in bellowing around us; but the Senhor P—— assured me those were only demonstrations of joy at the return
of our horses, their companions. He called the shepherd, a
little mulatto of about eleven years, and whose dress consisted
of a large linen bag held around his hips by a cord, and raised
in front like a pair of underdrawers. The boy called his beasts,
and we could at last pass through the *boiada*, not without heart-
beating on my part. I could never get myself habituated to this
thing. Each time in coming or going that I found myself in the
midst of all these horned beasts, there was always a certain
emotion (enough cause, besides); for, one day when we were
about to start, a furious bull sprang toward the horse on which
my son was seated. I uttered a cry, and the herder, who fortunately was near, immediately threw the lasso over the neck of
the beast, which stopped short and fell on its knees.

Nothing [is] more curious than to see the negroes throw
the lasso; it is done with such dexterity that one is stupefied. It
is in this manner that one takes in the meadows the horses or
mules that one wishes to ride; and when, having returned, after having given them a handful of oats, the saddle is removed,
they return to the pasture without giving them further care
until the day that one requires their service again. They re-

ceive no rations but on the day when they are ridden. The Sao Jozé *fazenda* had only twenty-five [approximately one hundred and twenty] negroes and negresses to do the plantation work. Hardly had we stepped in when we were led to our rooms, where a bath *à la cachaça* (molasses brandy) was awaiting us, destined for regaining our strength. The *fazendeiro*, upon arriving, had completely changed face; his countenance, usually so amiable during the whole trip, had suddenly become severe and hard; he hardly said, "How do you do!" to a Frenchwoman who was his housekeeper, and scarcely answered the slaves of the plantation, who pressed around him to ask for his benediction or blessing. Our bath taken, the bell rang for dinner, and we then appeared in the dining-room, with its old, blackened walls, opening on an inner court, dirty enough. This room, long and narrow, had for furniture nothing but a large square table, around which wooden benches were ranged. On the table was seen the traditional *feijoada*, dishes filled with manioca, a large platter of rice, and two chickens, as well as bananas and oranges. This is about the usual Brazilian dinner to be found in the interior, where fresh meat is a rare thing.

We had brought from the city white bread for two or three days, after which we had therefore to do without it until the following Saturday, when a negro was sent on horseback to a little neighboring place called Santo Aleixo, which possessed a baker who kindly baked once a week.

Dinner over, the host called his *feitor* (foreman), an old negro called Ventura, whom I yet can see with his good face, honest and grave. He came escorted by two other large darkies, who were his aides; all three had for clothing nothing but a coarse linen shirt, worn over their trousers, made of sailcloth. Over their shoulders were thrown some sort of tatters, which, in by-gone days, might have been coats or overcoats. In one hand they rolled their hats of coarse straw, while the other was ornamented by a long, stout stick, and Ventura held the *chicote* (whip), insignia of his command. Besides, each one carried an immense cutlass (a kind of little sword), with which the slaves help themselves to cut sugar-cane, or make their way through the woods. They placed themselves, all three, standing before their master, in an angle of the room, which was scarcely lit up by two candles burning in glass panes placed on the large silver chandelier. This scene has remained present in my memory in its minutest details, for to a Parisienne it did not lack strangeness.

These are the questions which were set by the master, in a short and hard tone, and the answers of the slaves, pronounced in a humble and frightened manner:—

"What has been planted this week?"

"Rice, senhor."

"Begun to cut the sugar-cane?"

"Yes, master; but the *rio*" (the river) "has overflowed, and we must repair the canals."

"Send twenty negroes over there to-morrow morning. What more?"

"Henriques has escaped."

"The *cachorro*" (the dog)! "Has he been caught?"

"*Sim*" (yes), "senhor, he is in the *tronco*" (in irons).

"Give him twenty blows with the lash, and put the iron collar around his neck."

"Yes, senhor. A troop of *porcas do mato*" (wild boars) "are ravaging all the *batatas* plantation, and a jaguar has been seen yesterday near the torrent: we ought to have guns."

"You shall have three this evening. Is this all?"

"Yes, senhor."

"*L'engenho* [*O engenho*]" (mill in which the manioca flour and sugar are made) "is to begin work to-morrow: is it in condition?"

"Yes, senhor."

"Very well. Call the negroes now for prayer."

We then all proceeded to the parlor, a room ordinarily placed in the middle of the house, lighted only by three large doors leading onto the veranda, which is in some way the real drawing-room of the hot countries.

The master rang a heavy bell, then called, in a formidable voice, "*Salta para a resa [reza]!*" (Hurry up for prayer).

Night had almost come. Oxen and horses were sleeping in the meadows. Before the house, and all around it, ranged in circle, were the *sauzales [senzalas]* (negro cabins), to the number of seventy about.

At the master's call, one saw rising up out of the dusk these sort of phantoms; each one came out of their cabin, a sort of hut made of clay and mud, with dried banana leaves for roofing, a gloomy abode, where the water penetrates when it rains, where the wind blows

Mulattress of the "Fazenda"

from everywhere, and from where a most dreadful smoke arises at the hour when the negro gets his supper, for the cabin has neither chimney nor window, so that the fire is made with a fagot, oftentimes green, which is lighted in the centre of the cabin.

The negroes cross the meadow and ascend one by one the two flights of stairs to the veranda, where a sort of cupboard had been opened, forming an altar in one of the corners. Here it was that the miseries of slavery appeared to me in all their horror and hideousness. Negresses covered in rags, others half naked, having as covering only a handkerchief fastened behind their back and over their bosoms, which scarcely veiled their throats, and a calico skirt, through whose rents could be seen their poor, scraggy bodies; some negroes, with tawny or besotted looks, came and kneeled down on the marble slabs of the veranda. The majority carried on their shoulders the marks of scars which the lash had inflicted; several were affected with horrible maladies, such as elephantiasis, or leprosy. All this was dirty, repulsive, hideous. Fear or hate, that is what could be read on all these faces, which I never have seen smile.

Four candles were lighted, and the two subordinate overseers placed themselves on the steps of the altar, where the Christ appeared, in the centre of four vases. These two negroes officiated after their own fashion; they had retained a smattering of Latin, which a chaplain, formerly at the plantation, had taught them, and then added their own most picturesquely, which served as a beginning to the litany of saints. After the *Kyrie eleison* they begin to sing in unison, *Santa Maria, mai de Deos, ora pro nobis!* Then all the saints in paradise followed, to whom they thought fit to add this, *Santa Pè de cana, ora pro nobis!* (Holy Foot, made of sugar-cane, pray for us!) Finally their singing ended with this heart-rending cry, which they all gave, prostrating themselves, their faces on the ground, *Miserere nobis!* This cry touched me to the inmost recesses of my heart, and tears streamed silently from my eyes, while, after the devotions, the negroes filed past us one by one in asking our benediction, to which each white person must reply, "I bless thee."

Prayers were held every Saturday evening. I could never listen to it without remaining profoundly impressed. The aspect of these miseries and these sufferings, and that cry of despair, which seemed to me to rise way up to God,—all this was striking, and of a horrible beauty, even from the artistic point of view.

The following day scenes not less sad awaited me. Having been awakened at four o'clock in the morning by the great bell in the veranda, which the *feitor* was ringing for the rising up of the negroes, I wished to witness these proceedings, and jumped out of my bed.

Day was scarcely dawning in the horizon, a soft and melancholy color was enveloping the landscape. From the summit of the mountain, in the rear of the *fazenda*, a beautiful cascade was unrolling its sheets of silvery water, and this mountain was covered with wild woods, where fruits and flowers interlaced each other in charming confusion.

From the other side, in front of the house, immense pastures could be seen, where more than a hundred head of cattle were collected. The oxen were still sleeping.

Some of the negroes began to come out of their cabins. If one of them was late in appearing, old Ventura would shake his big whip in crying out, "*O Patife! puxa para fora!*" (O good-for-nothing, get out!)

Then three gangs, each of about twenty-five negroes and negresses, were formed: one was under the direction of Ventura, and took the way to the *matto* (woods); the second proceeded to the plantations with one of the subordinate superintendents; and the third drove immense wagons with wheels of solid wood, yoked by four oxen, and was getting ready to cut the sugar-cane, which the wagons were to carry back. One of the little shepherds in his turn collected all the oxen, the second followed him with a flock of sheep; the field gates were opened, and all this human live stock started with the rest for work.

Four dairy cows alone were left for the needs of the house, and at six o'clock we were served to a bowl of milk, the like of which I have never drunk anywhere, on account of the exquisite perfume which is given it by the Indian pears, *pitangas*, mangoes, and above all the aromatic plants of which the cows are very fond, and with which they feed themselves in the woods. This is what our animals know nothing of. When, sometimes, they are let loose in our pastures, hardly can they find a bit of grass; while nothing is funnier to see in Brazil than a cow plucking fruit from the tree whose branches she bends.

Many a time while out horseback riding have we met them in this occupation, while the mares and colts in freedom were chasing each other through the fields, executing the most graceful of leaps.

The *moleque* (darky) who enjoys the best health at the *fazenda* is, without question, the *vaqueiro* (cow-keeper), because he does not forget himself, and milks the cows for his proper [own] benefit far from the eye of his master. It has also happened sometimes that with four cows there would hardly be the necessary milk for the house, the negroes awarding themselves a little too much, and the cow-keeper would be punished; yet when one would see the food given these poor unfortunates, one could not blame them for trying to make up.

At nine o'clock the bell would ring again; it was rung for the negroes' breakfast, and I had the curiosity to be present at the distribution of the rations. There are always two cooks at a plantation,—one for the whites and one for the blacks,—and there are even two kitchens. I repaired to the large smoky room which served for the darkies' kitchen, and there I saw two negresses having before them two immense caldrons, one of them containing *feijoes* and the other *angú* (a dough made of manioca flour and boiling water). Each slave soon arrived, gourd in hand. The cook would pour in a large ladleful of *feijoes*, adding a little piece of *carne secca* of the poorest quality, as also a little manioca flour sprinkled over all; the other one distributed the *angú* to the old men and children. The poor slaves would leave with this, murmuring in a low tone that the meat was rotten, and that there was not enough.

Our dogs would certainly not have eaten such food. The little darkies of three or four years, entirely naked, were returning with their rations of *feijoes*, which their delicate stomachs could hardly digest; also did they nearly all have large stomachs, enormous heads, and lank arms and legs,—in short, all the signs of the rickets. It caused pity to see them; and I never understood, from a speculative stand-point even, that these merchants of human flesh did not take better care of their merchandise. Happily, I was assured that it was not thus everywhere, and that in several plantations the slaves were very well treated. I wish to believe it; for myself, I tell what I have seen.

One day while I was out walking a little far out in the plantation, I was accosted by a very young negress who came to ask me to intercede for her to her master, so that she might be freed of the chain she was carrying. In saying this, she lifted up her coarse linen skirt, and showed me a ring riveted around her ankle, to which was attached a heavy chain carried from her waist. Here is the conversation I had with her, I immediately wrote down textually:—

"I am very willing," said I to the poor slave, "to ask your pardon, but what bad action have you committed to have deserved this punishment? Did you steal?"

"No, senhora, I fled."

"And why did you flee?"

"Because the slave must flee from slavery always."

"And if your chain is taken from you, then you will flee again?"

"No; because I see that the white man is always stronger than we are, and that I would again be caught and martyrized. This chain breaks me down."

"Then you promise me that if I obtain your pardon, you will never attempt to fly?"

"I promise it," replied the poor African woman, in a low tone.

"How old are you?"

"I do not know."

"What! more or less, you do not know how old you are?

"No."

"Is it long since you were brought to Brazil?"

"Sugar-cane has been cut five times since then."

"Do you remember your country?"

"Always!" she replied, with a wild and passionate accent.

"You did not work in your native land?"

"No: when I had pounded the rice for the repasts, I danced and sang the rest of the day."

"Do you remember the dances of your country?"

"Do I remember them? Every night, after the superintendents sleep, we get up and dance our dances till morning."

"And if some one bought you, to give you your liberty, you would return to Africa?"

"Yes, if I can find the way, for one must cross much water to get there."

"Have hope, my child: you will have better days."

I came home that day feeling sad, and did not have much trouble in obtaining the pardon of the young negress; for a Brazilian never refuses a pardon asked for a slave, especially if it is asked by a woman, and that woman happens to be the *madrinha* (godmother) of one of his children; the title of godfather and godmother being nearly a tie of relationship in Brazil. Also, when I took leave to make a year's travel in France, Senhor P——, who accompanied us to the steamer, asked me what he could do to make himself agreeable to his *comadre*.*

"Not to beat your slaves any more," I answered him.

He promised it to me, and during a year religiously kept his promise; only he begged me, upon my return, never to ask him such a thing again, because his slaves would be lost forevermore.

Among all my horseback rides through the interior of the country one has remained engravened in my memory. Our friend, the *fazendeiro*, P——, wished to take us one day to a

---

*Co-mother, or godmother as viewed by the godchild's parents—Ed.

cotton mill which an American from the North had just established in a little place called Santo Aleixo, hardly six miles distant from the Sao Jozé plantation. This was a complete novelty for the Brazilians to see a factory in their country. As for me, the factory did not interest me, but the excursion through the woods enchanted me.

We started at eight o'clock in the morning, I mounting the horse of the senhora, as the horse was called, and which had but a slight defect, that of freeing himself of her who mounted him, when he felt a woman's long skirt on his side, so that when he was passing near a ravine he would make a little side movement, in the intention of throwing his rider, if she was not firm in the saddle. Knowing he had this little trick, I was in the habit of holding him strongly in check during these delicate occasions; seeing this, he lost, day by day, his roguish idea, and we were the best friends in the world. My husband mounted a large red horse, called the horse of the *cidade* (of the city). Why? I ignore it. [I don't know.] This horse had such a hard trot that he was never given to a woman. As to the proprietor, he always had his gray mule, on which he seemed to sit as in his arm-chair. Holding in his right hand a large umbrella to shield him from the sun, he scarcely deigned to hold the reins. Finally, my son came riding a little pony, which had been given him, sitting more solidly in his saddle than any of us, and enduring six hours' riding without flinching.

To begin with, we had to cross a wood where myriads of birds flew off at our approach, and where the monkeys' sharp cries were heard. How enchanting was this road. The Senhor P—— suddenly called to me, however,—"Stop your horse: a serpent crosses the road!"

In reality we saw a little serpent of changeable red color, which was warming itself in the sun, and disappeared at the sound of our approach.

"He hasn't a very wicked look, your little serpent," I said to our host.

"It is the coral serpent," he replied: "one of those whose sting is most dangerous."

We continued on our way, and finally arrived before a little river.

"We are going to cross it," said our host.

"How?" I replied. "I don't see any bridge."

"Why, simply on our horses: gather up well your riding-skirt, lift your left limb over your saddle in tailor-fashion, give the reins to your horse,—don't be frightened,—and follow my mule, who will find her way."

It was done in this manner: our horses began to get into the water up to their bodies, then to their chests, and finally, in a moment, they lost their footing and swam a few seconds with their riders on their back.

I was not greatly reassured. The horses, to cut the current at a certain part where it was very rapid, were always going sideways, and it seemed to me as if the opposite shore was disappearing, instead of getting nearer to us.

This lasted about six minutes at the most, yet it seemed long to me; but I have kept a charming souvenir of it,—this little river, bordered by plants and trees of all kinds, with its limpid and flowing water, that sky so beautifully blue, and the warm sun over our heads, in the midst of all this, our little caravan crossing the *rio* on horseback. I see it all again, and am happy to have passed through these little experiences and con-templated such splendid landscapes.

Senhor P—— having begged us (my husband and I) to be godfather and godmother of his last child, this gave place—after the ceremony of baptism, which was held by a chaplain of the neighborhood—to one of the strangest feasts, which I will endeavor to describe.

We desired that the poor slaves should have their share in the day's festivities, and their master permitted us to treat them to a small keg of *cachaça*, authorizing them after this, at my request, to dance in the evening on the meadow.

It was a day of intermission of their labors. I will allow you to think whether they were happy and came to thank us.

The overseer then made the distribution of the *cachaça*, giving each one but a small glass at a time, and then the *batuco* [*batuque*] (negro's dance, accompanied with the clapping of hands) began. I wish I could give my readers an idea of this strange scene and of this wild dance. Let me try.

Large fires had been lit in the middle of the meadow. A negro of high stature, formerly king in his native country, soon appeared, armed with a long white wand,—sign apparent, to them, of his command. His head was ornamented with feathers of all colors, and little bells were fastened around his legs. Every one bowed himself down before him with respect, while he gravely walked about, dressed in this manner, filled with a supreme majesty. Near the king stood the two musicians who were to lead the *batuco*; one carried a kind of immense calabash, which contained six or seven of different sizes, over which were placed a very thin little board. With the aid of little sticks, which he manœuvred with great dexterity, the negro obtained dull sounds, the monotony of which seemed sooner to provoke sleep than anything else. The second musician, squatted on his heels, had before him a piece of the hollow trunk of a tree, over which a dried lambskin was stretched. He was beating in a melancholy way on this primitive drum to re-enforce the singing. Three or four groups of dancers soon came to place themselves in the centre of the circle, which was formed by all their companions. The negresses walked harmoniously, keeping time in waving their handkerchiefs and in giving themselves up to a most accentuated movement of the hips, while their dark partners were turning around them, skipping upon one foot with the most grotesque contortions, and the old musician was walking from one group to another, speaking and singing, while shaking his sticks with frenzy. He seemed, by his expressions, desirous of exciting them for the dance, while the assistants accompanied the *batuco* with clapping of hands, which accentuated the rhythm in a strange manner, and the king was promenading in a grave manner while shaking his bells.

The negroes were dripping, and yet the musicians did not cease running from one to the other and exciting them still more. The dance had arrived at such a degree of strange over-excitement, when suddenly calling was heard from the house: "*Feitor*, let all fires be extinguished, that all noise ceases, and that all the negroes return to their cabins!"

There was some murmuring among the poor slaves, but the overseer, armed with his whip and followed by his two assistants, soon restored order everywhere.

Not knowing to what to attribute this sudden disturbance in the festival, I hastily ascended to the house, where I found the proprietor perfectly pale, and having barricaded windows and doors around him. He seemed to me laboring under a certain excitement, whose cause I asked him.

He then told me that, while his comrades were dancing, a negro had entered the house, with drunken face, and vocifer-ating threats against his master, who immediately had him laid hold of, but who had understood that if his negroes became more excited by the *cachaça* and their national dance, his life might be in danger.

We were, in the number of whites, at the house, only Senhor P——, my husband, I, and a sort of housekeeper, who held the middle place between hostess and servant. What could we have done against one hundred and twenty infuriated negroes? I, a young wife without any experience then, who had the conscience of never having done but good to these unfortunates, did not understand the danger, and could not help myself laughing at the frightened face of the proprietor. Later on, in reflecting, I found his terror justified.

These national dances excite to such a degree these poor slaves, that they have been prohibited to them in the city. In spite of all this, however, they take place. At the risk of being cruelly beaten, the negroes go at night, when the whites are asleep, to dance on the beach in the moonlight. They assemble in groups of the same nationality, either Congo, Mozambique, or Minas; then, in dancing and singing, they forget their ills and servitude, and only remember their native country and the time that they were free.

Sometimes it has happened to me, having need of the services of my *mucama* (lady's-maid) in the night, to search for her in vain all over the house: she had gone to rejoin her brethren at the dance. Our doors, however, had been carefully locked. Little did it concern her: she passed through the window.

One of the strangest types on the plantation, assuredly, was the *feiticeiro* (sorcerer). This is how I made his acquaintance: I was sitting one morning in the veranda, lost in that region of thought which vast horizons plunge you into, when I saw returning from the wood one of the wagons which usually did not come back until the decline of day. I was yet more surprised that it had for its only load two negroes, one of whom was the overseer.

"O Ventura?" immediately called our host to him, "why do you return with Luiz?"

"Senhor, Luiz has been bitten by a serpent while cutting sugar-cane, and is vomiting blood."

"Has the sorcerer been called?"

"Yes, senhor: there he comes."

In effect [in fact], we soon saw a negro of very high stature appear, with frizzled white hair, who, it was said, was more than ninety years old, but who, however, still held himself firmly and straight. He was draped in a striped covering, carried a sort of hanging wallet at his side, and held a stick in his hand. His face was grave and pensive.

He went straight to the infirmary, where the sick negro had been put, closeted himself with him, made him drink a preparation of herbs of which he alone had the secret, and affirmed that he would cure the negro, on condition, nevertheless, that no woman must be allowed to enter the room of him whom he nursed, for seven days. Without this, he would not be responsible for him, he said; therefore, one was careful to send the negro's food only by men. The prescriptions of the sorcerer were carried out to the letter, and the negro was completely cured. Thereupon I wished to talk with the old sorcerer; and after having given him a few pennies for coffee and sugar, I asked him what were the plants he had made use of to cure the sting of the *jararaca*, one of the most dangerous serpents of Brazil.

"It is my secret," he said.

"Why don't you give it to the others?"

"I nurse them when they are ill: it is enough."

"But when you die?"

"All the worse for them. If they were good to me, I would gladly tell them the secrets I know; but they shun me, and teach their children to be afraid of me. I will take my secrets with me."

This was all that I could get. He was still called another time, for an ox who had *bicharia* (a bag full of worms).

The sorcerer approached the ox, which was lying down, applied to him, without doubt, also, some pulverized plant on the sick spot: the bag of worms fell almost instantly, and the animal was cured.

There was not a negro of the *fazenda* then who did not repeat that the sorcerer had only need to recite a few magical words, and immediately after the cure had been made.

The old negro had been right: in return for his science he reaped only ingratitude and abandonment; all shunned him, in almost crossing themselves, and the little mulattoes pressed against each other when he passed, whispering in each other's ears, "*Toma sentido! O feiticeiro!*" (Take care: there goes the sorcerer!)

As for me, it was always with pleasure that I conversed with him, and I regret sincerely to-day that I did not write down these original conversations, so simple and so instructive all at once; for the old darky, who had seen the reign of Dom Joañ VI,* knew many things although he had not learned to read and to write. It was in the grand book of nature that he had studied. What became of him?

He has died, without doubt all alone, in a corner of the forest, taking with him all the science so laboriously gathered in eighty-six years of existence.

Speaking of serpents also reminds me of an adventure which was the talk of Rio at this time.

One of the richest stock brokers of the country one day told at the stock exchange what had just happened to him.

For some time his little three-year-old daughter, who slept in the room next her parents, would wake up during the night in crying, and when she would be questioned as to the cause of her tears would cry, "*O bicho! O bicho!*" (the animal). One thought of nightmares; but the child grew pale, and would say from time to time, "*O bicho frio! frio!* [cold]" finally they became alarmed at the child's persistence in speaking of the *bicho*, so one night the father, armed with a pistol, placed himself upon duty, without light, near the child's bed. Towards midnight the little one began to move, and the father then perceived a serpent of the most dangerous kind lying next his child. He was careful not to frighten it, else it would sting the little one. The father rapidly carried off the child, and almost immediately killed the serpent. Since then the child has regained its bright color, and no longer says, "The beast is cold!"

When four years later, I returned for the second time to the Sao Jozé plantation, this time without the escort of our host, and starting with our two children, Paul and Maurice, the elder being twelve years old, and the younger scarcely sixteen months old, whom I still was nursing, we carried him,

*Dom João VI, regent and then king of Portugal, who moved to Rio with his court when Napoleon's armies invaded Portugal and who ruled the Portuguese empire from Brazil from 1808 to 1821—Ed.

each in turn, in our saddles, my husband and I; and most frequently it was our mulatto Fernando (one of the most successful types, who played the guitar, and perfumed himself from head to feet with cologne when called for my service) who carried him on his shoulders, in following on foot. On this account we journeyed very slowly; and when the day was beginning to decline, the page declared to us that we were still three hours distant from the plantation, and that we must cross, to get there, a kind of swamp, most dangerous at night.

Then I thought of the serpents, of the *oncas*,* and became frightened to find myself journeying at night with my two children. I told my husband that I thought it imprudent to continue our journey under such conditions, and as for me I decided to stop in a *rancho* (a kind of shelter with a roof, with a manger for animals) sooner than to expose my sons to so many dangers. The page then told me that in going a little out of our way we would come within a half-hour to a plantation where we probably could pass the night. I accepted this suggestion with eagerness.

We quickened our pace, and in a very short time indeed we reached the plantation of the *vis-condessa de P—— G——*. It was time, for obscurity [darkness] was enveloping us from everywhere.

Having arrived at the entrance of the plantation, we asked to see the superintendent, who was a white man, who really sooner was called the *administrador*.

He soon arrived, and we told him of our embarrassment, in asking for hospitality for the night. He eagerly accorded it to us in the name of his masters, who for years had not inhabited their *fazenda*. We therefore alighted, after having thanked him heartily. He then gave orders to have the guest chamber put in order for us, where I finally had the joy of seeing my

---

*Onça, any of various wildcats, pumas, or cougars—Ed.

two sons asleep, each in a separate bed, instead of being exposed in the forest to all kinds of dangers.

The *senhor administrador*, who had a smattering of knowledge, was charmed to see strangers who brought him news from the city, came and conversed with us while we ate our travelling supplies; then, towards eleven o'clock, he left us.

I had asked the negress who had attended to my room if she could get me a night-lamp. This was an unknown thing at the plantation, where oil for lighting had never entered. That which was brought me in its stead was a kind of rosin taper, the smoke of which would have suffocated us if we had not left all the inner doors of the apartment wide open. This taper, disagreeable as it was, however, did me great service, for hardly had I gotten in bed, worn out with fatigue, when I heard a little moving about the room. "They are mice," said I to myself; "in frightening them a little, they'll go away." So I knocked against the bed and the wall, hoping thus to get rid of them. Ah! well, yes! The moment I laid my head upon my pillow the noise increased, and I'll let you imagine what became of me when I saw, instead of mice, enormous rats (about the size of small cats), ornamented with long mustaches, which were crossing the room in gangs of eight or ten, to nibble the leavings of our supper.

I awakened my husband, to tell him of my fright.

"What do you want?" he replied, half asleep.

"This room has not been occupied for a long time, and the chicken and *pâté* have attracted all the rats of the place over here."

"What to do about it? Try not to think about it, and get asleep."

Get myself asleep in the midst of these horrid creatures! I didn't even think of it. I was afraid they'd get into our beds and bite my children; so I passed the whole night sitting up in my bed, knocking to frighten them away every time when I would see them coming towards us.

That was the manner in which I rested after a day of great fatigue.

It was not until the dawn of day that they kindly left, and scarcely allowed me an hour's rest, for at five o'clock we were all up, so as to avoid the great heat.

I had noticed, the evening before, a young woman, white, or rather yellow, with large eyes darkly circled, badly combed hair, who walked barefooted, dressed in a miserable skirt, and a child at one hand, another in arms, and I had suspected that it might well be the wife of the *administrador*, who, however, had himself fine linen, a proper suit of clothes, and a certain varnish of books and science.

I had communicated my suspicions to my husband, who, like all the husbands in the world, did not give it credence, and had even plagued me of that mania all women have, of seeing romances and dramas in everything.

Well, before leaving I wished to have a clear conscience about it. I asked for some bowls of milk, and it was this woman, accompanied by the two children, who served them to us. I resolved thereupon to satisfy my curiosity; and while my children were eating and our horses were being saddled, noticing on her face the traces of great suffering, "You seem sad, madam," I said to her.

"I am very unhappy, senhora," she replied.

"Are you not the wife of the *administrador?*"

"To my sorrow."

"How?"

"He treats me badly. Those are his mulattresses," she continued, in pointing towards one, "who are the real senhoras of the plantation; for them my husband overwhelms me with outrages."

"How can you live with him? Leave him."

She looked at me in utter astonishment.

"Leave my husband!" she uttered. "And by what should I live?"

"You will work."

"I do not know how to earn money; and my children?"

"The father will be obliged to bring them up; but you can leave them no longer with such a sight under their eyes: a mother cannot allow herself to be outraged before her children. If they are to respect you, make yourself respected."

The poor woman listened to me with all ears, trying to understand, and opening wide her large eyes.

"That's all very well for you Frenchwomen, who know how to earn your bread," she finally said; "but we, to whom nothing has been taught, we are obliged to be the servants of our husbands."

"Well, do what you like; but when you will have suffered enough, and find yourself at the end of your strength, remember the Frenchwoman who passed a night at the plantation, and come to her: she will give you the means of living by your work. Here is my address."

Thereupon I jumped into the saddle. The wife of the superintendent thanked me by look, and accompanied me to the gate of the plantation; she remained there, looking after me fixedly as long as she could see something of me.

I could well see that I had enlightened this soul, and opened new longings before her.

Daybreak was appearing and began to lighten a little the dark foliage of the woods; nature awakened, still enveloped in the mist, and the dew was sprinkled over the ground. The *senhor administrador* came to give us his adieus, in wishing us God-speed. I involuntarily looked back. After what I knew, he gave me the horrors.

When we arrived on the borders of the *fazenda*, we found the mulattresses of the day before looking haughty and cynical, who wished to see in broad daylight the French lady and her husband.

They gave me, for a last adieu, a look full of hate, yet bowing all the same when I passed; and I, from my side, acknowledged it by an easy bow, into which I put all the disdain and disgust which they inspired.*

Then, taking a little gallop, we started towards the Sao Jozé plantation, at which we arrived two hours later.

Three months later, my door-bell rang. It was the Senhora Maria, the wife of the *administrador*, who came, with one of her children on her arm, asking me to fulfil the promise I had made her; so I took her into my home as house-keeper, to over-look the negro servants, and to take charge of the household linen.

To say that in the end she repaid me with the most profound ingratitude teaches nothing new to my readers. What matters it? My end had been gained: I had developed in her soul the sentiment of human dignity, and had taught her how to earn her daily bread; I had raised her up morally, and cured her physically. The Senhora Maria has never been able to forget me, this I am sure of.

*This English translation by Adèle Toussaint-Samson's daughter Emma omits the earlier paragraph in which Adèle describes those mulattas as trying to attract her husband the previous night—Ed.

PART IV
Among the People

—◦◦◦—

*O*ne must acknowledge that our country was singularly represented in Brazil during the twelve years that I inhabited it.

Having met several times on my way, when I first arrived, a tall, thin man, the carrier of a high white cravat, out of which his bird-like head seemed to emerge as out of a cornet, who went his way brushing against the walls, always poorly dressed, and shod in rubbers, under a tropical heat, I asked who this poor, abashed being was, who seemed begging everybody's pardon for the audacity of his stature,—the only one he had,— besides which, he tried to dissimulate, in humbly bending before everybody.

I was told that it was Mr. T—— [Théodore Marie Taunay], our consul at Rio, a very good man, it was said, of whom the French could justly be proud. At this reply, I was provoked with myself for the bad impression his sexton-like bearing had given me, and resolved to modify my first judgment over our consul.

Still, do what I might, I always found in this man something of the Jesuit, which would not agree with me. I had occasion later to judge this excellent man, who did not in any manner hold up the interests of honest people, and filled out his functions of consul in a very odd manner, as you will see.

A lady friend of mine, for example, having been left a widow, and without resources, had set about to give French and drawing lessons to support the two sons which her husband had left her. The poor woman, rising at dawn, scarcely

taking five hours' rest, managed in this way, good and bad together, to have both ends meet. One day she went to see
Mr. T——, asking him to help her get the sum of two hundred francs, which a pupil of hers, a woman of a certain class,
owed her for a long time, and which she refused to settle. She
was in this part of her story when our consul, interrupting her
suddenly, said,—

"Have you any debts, madam?"

"No, sir; thanks to my incessant work and my extreme
economy, I haven't any," she replied.

"You are then far happier than the person of whom you
speak," said the holy man in a soft voice.

"What!" retorted my friend: "you find that I am happier
than this lady, who denies herself nothing, while I deny myself
everything, and who remains *nonchalantly* stretched all day on
her *marquesa*" (couch made of rushes on which the Brazilians
sleep during the great heat), "while I have to run about in sunshine or rain?"

"She has debts, and you have none: you are, assuredly, the
most happy one."

"Then she it is whom you pity, and you find it just that my
work should be unpaid?"

"I do not find it just, dear lady; only, I tell you, you are the
least to be pitied, since you have no debts."

And this was all she could get out of it; he did not answer
her otherwise to all her arguments; and this good man did not
interest himself in the least in her affair.

Another time, it was my turn to go and find him for something similar.

A carriage-maker, in the sale of a carriage to my husband,
had made an act of dishonesty, and cheated his customer, so
to say. My husband protested, and wished to have the carriage
appraised before paying the price agreed upon. When I entered the consulate, Mr. T——nearly prostrated himself before me, which made me think it my duty to declare, at the

very soonest, my name and baptismal name, thinking he took me, perhaps, for some empress in disguise.

After I had explained the whole matter to him, "What do you propose to do?" he asked me.

"But, sir, I do not know, since it is precisely what I come to ask you about."

"Well, my advice would be to hush up the matter, and not give it consequences."

"Yet, you see that we have been cheated?"

"Without question."

"You wish us to pay, all the same?"

"Assuredly: you are honest people, and have your conscience for you; that must be sufficient to you."

"Not exactly."

"Besides, this amount is not of much consequence to you."

"I beg your pardon, sir."

"There! there! you're not so poor," he continued smilingly.

"Fortunately for us," I answered him; "for I see if we reckoned only upon your protection in this country, we might die of hunger."

Thereupon I took leave of this excellent man, who accompanied me [all the] way to the door, in continuing to bow in the lowest manner possible to him.

This was all I had obtained.

This extreme condescension for swindlers had given our consul many sympathies, you can imagine; the same as his affectation, in going out under a burning sun, wearing rubbers, under pretext of giving all to the poor, which had gained him the reputation of saintliness. But on solemn occasions, at the *Te Deum*, for this or that anniversary, when our navy would parade headed by music, and when one would perceive, in the midst of all these brilliant uniforms, all these decorations, all our waving flags, this tall, old man with the long neck, concealing himself behind some column, not daring to look any one in the face, and murmuring some confused sentences, one could not hardly help exclaiming, "It is a fact, the French have there a singular representative!"

As for our own minister, Mr. de St—— [Léonce de St. Georges], although he differed on all points with his consul, he represented France not less oddly than Mr. T—— in the interests of his compatriots.

He was short, stout, round like a ball; also was it said that between the two they completed the jumping-jack.

Mr. de St—— was nearing forty upon our arrival in Brazil. He must have been a very handsome fellow, and had the reputation of being very fond of the ladies. Married recently to a Brazilian lady, he occupied at Cattete a pretty villa, where every week he would give a little evening party. There, with the exception of the admiral, a few navy officers, and a Frenchwoman (formerly of a certain class) married to a rich Portuguese merchant as questionable as she, were received only Brazilians, which in no small measure contributed to discredit French society in the eyes of the natives. But what did it matter to our minister, of whom nothing of the Frenchman was left but the name?

One could not say that Mr. de St—— carried high the flag of France; but as the government of Brazil had not the smallest desire to declare war against us, it was found that the attitude of our minister had fortunately no importance whatever.

Owing, without doubt, to the exclusion of the French residents from the drawing-room of their minister, our compatriots were very little thought of at Rio Janeiro at this time. It must be said that the French colony consisted largely of working people, hair-dressers, and milliners, who had left their country poor, to come and seek their fortune in America, and that all these people did not shine too brightly by their manners or education.

However, there was also at Rio a small nucleus of well-educated persons,—artists, journalists, merchants,—who would have met each other with pleasure at the embassy of the representative of their country, and who could have given the inhabitants of Rio a better opinion of the French nation than that which they formed in Ouvidor Street, at their tailors or at their florists.

As the Brazilian ladies never went out alone in the streets at this epoch, one would meet only in the city the French ladies or English ladies, who, by the very fact of going out alone, would see themselves exposed to many adventures. Therefore the French ladies, were they married or not, could not step outside without seeing themselves assailed with compliments, ogled, and with *billets-doux*, in a style as cavalierly about as this: "Madam, I love you. Can you receive me at your house this evening?" Not more ceremony than this.

These gentlemen thought they had only to present themselves, and that, as the French ladies smiled pleasantly and conversed as easily with men as with women, their conquest was of the easiest. Happily more than one received of our fair compatriots some good lessons.

Some wagers were taken in the city in regard to a French lady, and it was the doctor with the skeleton, of whom I have already spoken, who, a sceptic in the highest degree, wagered for the ruin of our fair compatriot.

Immediately a handsome officer, very much smitten with the lady, began the campaign, showering upon her bouquets and *billets-doux*, through the intermediary of the blacks, whom he bribed, while another one, a not less charming cavalier, followed our "Parisienne" everywhere, and passed whole nights under her window. Lost labors! The lady mercilessly shut doors and windows in their faces, and returned their love-letters without answers. They, all abashed, returned each day to the doctor, telling their ill-success, who would tell them, "Do not lose courage, it is only a question of time."

However, at the end of two years, seeing their walks and labors at their own loss, they summoned the doctor to pay the wager he had lost; which did not prevent our Brazilian from repeating that he did not believe in the virtue of any woman in general, and the French ladies in particular.

It was not until long afterwards that our fair compatriot learned that she had been the subject of a wager, and doubly congratulated herself in having put these fops in their places.

I admit, as for me, that nothing has ever amused me so much as to see these Brazilians, so sure of their conquest, laughed at by our French ladies, who, as you know, in point of mockery or coquetry, can teach lessons to all the nations of the earth.

By means of little lessons of this kind the Americans of the South have at last understood that there are women who, because they go alone on foot, under a scorching sun, earning their living in teaching, are but the more honorable, and they begin by no longer saying, with that air of profound disdain, "It is a madame!" because more than one madame has taught them how to behave.

As for the Brazilian ladies, penned up as they are by their husbands in the enclosure of their houses, in the midst of their children and their slaves, never going out unaccompanied to either Mass or processions, one must not imagine, on that account, that they are more virtuous than others, only they have the art of appearing so.

Everything is done mysteriously in these impenetrable abodes, where the lash has made the slave as silent as the tomb. Under the cloak of the family even, many things are hidden. All this *is*, or at least *was* (for since several years the Brazilian ladies go out alone),—all this is the fruit of the sequestration imposed upon women. Besides, the appearances are so well guarded that one must live years in the land to begin to know the inner life of these homes, of such patriarchal customs and habits, at first sight, where frequently three generations live together under the same roof in the most perfect concord; for one must say, in this regard, that the Brazilians are much our superiors. They have found the secret of uniting in the same house son-in-law, mother-in-law, daughter-in-law, without there ever being conflict. That ferocious hatred for the mother-in-law, which is at present professed in France, is unknown over there. One does not believe that, by the simple fact of marrying her daughter or her son, a mother who has been good and devoted all her life can suddenly become a monster. One has the greatest respect for the father and the mother.

When the Brazilian comes home he finds in his house a dutiful wife, whom he treats as a spoilt child, bringing her dresses, jewels, and ornaments of all kinds; but this woman is not associated to him, neither in his business, his preoccupations, nor his thoughts. It is a doll whom he dresses for an occasion, and who, in reality, is but the first slave of the house; although the Brazilian of Rio Janeiro is never brutal, and exercises his despotism in a manner almost gentle. All this besides, as I have already said, is undergoing complete changes.

The Brazilian ladies of to-day, educated in French or English boarding schools, have little by little taken our habits and our manner of seeing; so that very gradually they acquire their liberty. Then, as their intelligence is very quick, I think that in a short time they will have surpassed their teachers.

It is in the interior of the country, whose roads are impassable but on donkey-back, and which render communication with the capital very difficult, that one can still study all these customs of Portuguese or Spanish origin. Likewise, when you arrive in a *fazenda*, you never perceive the senhora, while she always has the means of seeing the stranger without their ever being aware of it. The *mascatoes* [*mascates*] (pedlers) have alone the privilege of being introduced near the lady of the house, and it is one of the grand events at the *fazenda* when the *mascato* comes. One must see him open his boxes and spread out before the *dona du* [*da*] *casa* (lady of the house) and her slaves the pieces of *chita* (printed calico), of *cassa* (muslin), of *cambraia* (cambric), the *fitas* (ribbons) of all colors, the *joias* (jewelry) of all makes. Mulattresses and negresses stand there with staring eyes and open mouth, wishing to buy all, with a *pataca* (sixteen cents) as their sole fortune, and always ending with the purchase of a simple kerchief.

The *mascato* is petted in secret by the negresses of the *fazenda*, who do not treat him cruelly, for little, if he wishes; but he is badly treated enough by the master of the house, who knows him to be a thief generally, and takes care to have the silver guarded when he sees him appear. However, he is given, like everybody, the hospitality of the night in the guest chamber, a room opening on the veranda of the house and not differently connected with any other apartments.

When you come to ask for hospitality, this room is always open to you, and a negress comes and brings you your bath, which every Brazilian is accustomed to take before going to bed, the same as the *feijoada* or the rice for your supper. When the traveller is of a certain class, the *fazendeiro* even has the kindness of sending his bath to him by the handsomest slave of the house.

The Brazilian is very hospitable; his table is open to all. I know of one who has his office in town, where he receives all who wish to come and dine with him, which makes his cook prepare a dinner for twenty or thirty persons daily. In our countries this seems princely. At Rio Janeiro it is not even noticed. Likewise, the stinginess of our habits and our boards [dinner tables] greatly surprise the South Americans when they come to France.

One of the opinions most generally accredited to the Brazilian lady is that she is lazy and remains unoccupied all day. One is mistaken: the Brazilian lady does nothing herself, but has others do it; she takes great pride in never being seen in any occupation whatever. However, when one is admitted into her intimacy, one finds her in the morning, her bare feet in *tamancas*, a dressing-gown of muslin for dress, presiding at the making of *doces* (preserves of all sorts), of the *cocada* (cocoa jelly), and arranging them on the *taboleiro* (large wooden platter) of her negresses or negroes, who soon leave to sell in the city the *doces*, the fruits, the vegetables of the plantation.

They gone, the senhoras prepare the sewing for the mulattresses; for nearly all the clothes of the children, of the master and mistress are cut and sewn at home. Then there are also napkins and handkerchiefs made in *crivo* point [embroidery], which are sent to be sold, like the rest. Each one of the slaves, called *ganho*, must bring back to his mistress a certain designated sum at the end of each day, and many are beaten when they return without this sum. This is what constitutes the pocket-money of the Brazilian ladies, and allows them to satisfy their whims.

They receive from France fashion plates, which they try to copy; but the majority have their dresses made by the great French dress-makers, where the least expensive ball dress costs from fifteen to eighteen hundred francs.

As I was saying a little while ago, a Brazilian lady would blush to be caught in any occupation whatever, for they profess the greatest disdain for all who work. The pride of the South American is extreme. Everybody wants to be master, no one wishes to serve. One admits, in Brazil, of no other profession but that of physician, lawyer, or wholesale merchant.

A Brazilian or Brazilian lady must never be surprised at anything whatever. When I would return from France with toilets of the latest fashion, I noticed the ladies looked at me secretly, by stealth, so as to study without appearing to do so the cut of my clothes, which not one of them would have acknowledged seeing for the first time. Should one have spoken to them about it, they would all have replied, unquestionably, "It is quite a long time since we wear that here."

One cannot say that the Brazilian ladies are beautiful, although, in general, they have beautiful eyes and splendid hair. There are certainly some very pretty ones; but the majority are either too thin or too stout, and what they lack above all is charm. They dress badly, generally ignoring elegant undress, and those thousand little nothings which make the Parisienne so bewitching. The expression of their faces is haughty and disdainful. They think by this that they give themselves the correct air, ignoring [not knowing] that, on the contrary, the true great ladies are simple, affable, and of the most exquisite politeness. They are willingly insolent enough, if one does not take the master hand over them. Money is the only superiority which they acknowledge; likewise, the most eminent artist is little thought of if he has not a cent. One should see the manner in which the natives say, in speaking of some one who is not rich, "*Coitadinho dèellel [dele] Coitado!*" It is untranslatable. It means, poor unfortunate! But it is full of a compassion mixed with disdain, which we cannot render in French.

You are only considered in Brazil by your clothes, by the number of your slaves, etc.; but, besides, you may be a little dishonest, without its being shocking the least in the world. One generally speaks of a man who has made his fortune in little ways not the most honest, *Soube arrangear [arranjar] se* (He knew how to arrange matters); or else, *Entende de negocios* (He understands business).

Extreme probity is a coin which has very little circulation in the land, so that one is thoroughly surprised to see people make much ado about it, and that the Brazilians are quite disposed to look upon those who consider it before all as dupes or as lunatics.

And yet this nation has done that which the French could not have done. It has brought up the child which Dom Pedro I* (after the Constitution had been proclaimed) intrusted to it to some day make its Emperor, and of this child it has made an honest man, a scholar, a liberal Emperor.

*Pedro I, Emperor from 1822 until his forced abdication in 1831, gave Brazil the constitution of 1824, which would remain in effect until the reign of his son, Pedro II, came to an end in 1889 with the establishment of a republic—Ed.

Dom Pedro II gives his subjects the example of goodness; and when one thinks in what a centre of corruption he has been brought up, one must give him double credit for it. The earnestness of his tastes and studies is not either an ordinary thing in Brazil, where every man conceals under a grave exterior the greatest frivolity.

The Emperor of Brazil speaks seven languages, Portuguese, Latin, Spanish, Italian, French, English, German, and last of all he has learned Hebrew. The science that he prefers above all others is, by what one is told, astronomy; likewise has he taught this science to his two daughters. After he visited France for the first time he left us the highest opinion of him as a scholar; and in the second journey which he made through our country he became thoroughly known.* He alone, who had abolished slavery† and endowed his people with all progress and large liberty, could allow himself to come in the midst of our young republican students; so fully did his conscience tell him that there was nothing to fear from them, for he was the most liberal of all. At the Théâtre Français he was seen applauding with enthusiasm all the *tirades* upon fatherland and liberty which are to be found in "Jean Dacier," a play written especially and acted by Coquelin.‡ A new Peter the Great, the Emperor of Brazil has travelled through all lands, borrowing from each what he thought might be useful to his father-land. Likewise, Brazil, since twenty years, is walking in giant strides; it is furrowed now by railways; it has schools of all kinds; painters and musicians are beginning to reveal themselves; the press is free, the Constitution respected, and the Brazilians give the example of a liberty without license, allied to a profound love for their Emperor.

*Pedro II's visit to Europe from April 1873 to June 1874 included much time spent in Paris. He again visited Paris from April to June 1877—Ed.

†A reference to the Law of the Womb, not the complete abolition of slavery, which occurred in 1888. See note on page 46—Ed.

‡Either Benoît Constant Coquelin (1841–1909) or Ernest Coquelin (1848–1909), the leading French actors of their day—Ed.

Emperor's Palace at San Cristovas [São Cristóvão]

What is most surprising is, that, in a country so full of pride, where the smallest merchant thinks himself a power, the Emperor is assuredly the most accessible of all his subjects. There is no need of asking an audience, to be admitted to his presence: he receives every Thursday, at his palace of San Christovo [São Cristóvão] (*see engraving*), those who wish to speak with him.

One awaits him in a long gallery, which the Emperor crosses at a certain given hour. There each one in turn explains what brought him hither. He seizes very rapidly what is told him, has a prodigious memory, and replies very briefly in the language of the person who speaks to him. The very poorest people are admitted to the palace.

Each one must kiss the hand of the Emperor in arriving and in taking leave; for, whatever may have been said, kissing the hand still exists in Brazil. It is the only established etiquette. For my part, I have often pitied Dom Pedro II, to be obliged to abandon his aristocratic hand to dirty people, whose breath alone could have been able to communicate to him some bad sickness; for what is curious is that custom obliges one, in kissing the hand of the Emperor, to draw off one's glove and touch his with the naked hand.

To give an idea with what facility one enters the Emperor's palace, here is an authentic story, which was told me by one of the ladies at court:—

One day when the princesses were in their study (or schoolroom) with the Countess de Barral,* their governess, and Mlle. Templier, their teacher, a valet came and announced the Archduke of Austria, later the unfortunate Emperor Maximilian.[†] The prince excuses himself for coming thus, without previously having solicited the favor of being received by their Highnesses, and tells, in smiling, that in leaving his carriage he entered the palace without being questioned, without even meeting a guard on his way. He had stepped straight forward, much surprised, not meeting any one; then finally, a lackey had appeared, whom he asked for the Emperor.

He was told that the latter was away on a two-days' visit with the Empress, but that the princesses were at home, and that they would be notified.

"By whom then is the emperor guarded?" continued the grand duke.

"By the love of his people, your Highness," answered him the Countess de Barral.

Truly, this does honor to the nation and to the sovereign!

I had the honor of being admitted twice to some intimate little *soirées* given by the imperial princesses, who had kindly asked me to arrange, or rather to disarrange, a play of Racine's,[‡] *Les Plaideurs*, so that they could represent [perform] it; and I must say that I have always seen the greatest simplicity reign

---

*Luísa Magarida Portugal de Barros—Ed.

[†]Installed as emperor of Mexico (1864–1867) by Napoleon III of France. After the French withdraw their support, his life was ended by a republican firing squad in 1867—Ed.

[‡]Jean Racine (1639–1699), the author of classic French tragedies—Ed.

at the court, where the Emperor and Empress—one can say it—give the example of the greatest virtues. I can say all this now, without being taxed [accused] as flattering, since my compatriots have been able to judge the Emperor for themselves, and have seen that I exaggerate nothing.

The life of the Empress is passed concentrated in her family and charity; still the imperial couple cannot do all the good they wish, because the sum allotted the emperor by the House [imperial household] is not enormous. He deprives himself, therefore, to give.

One of the most distinguished persons at the court is assuredly the Countess de Barral, a Brazilian lady, educated in France, and married to one of our greatest French names. She it is who has directed the education of the two princesses. Their teacher, Mlle. Templier, has also been a French lady, recommended to the court of Brazil by Queen Amalie.*

Thanks to their directress, *grande dame* in verity, and to their teacher, a person perfectly recommendable and highly educated, the two princesses have had the very best education, and have become two charming women. One of them, married to the Duke of Saxe, had died, unfortunately, a few years ago.

The imperial princess [Isabel], the one who is to succeed the Emperor, and whose husband is the Count d'Eu, alone is living. All the male children of the Emperor and Empress of Brazil died at an early age; but the imperial princess has given birth to two sons, who are the hope of Brazil.

To return to the Brazilian ladies: when they lose their husbands they must remain eight days confined to a room whose blinds are all carefully shut. It is there that, plunged in the deepest obscurity [darkness], they receive the visits of their relatives and friends. Once widows, the women never leave off

---

*D. Amélia, second wife of Pedro I and empress of Brazil from 1829 until 1831 and the abdication of her husband—Ed.

mourning, unless they remarry; only, at the end of several years, it is more half mourning that they wear; thus the widows must never dress themselves but in black, purple, or high blue, which is considered as a color of mourning in the land.

During the first days which follow the death, it is customary at Rio Janeiro to expose the deceased dressed in his best clothes in the middle of the drawing-room, where each one comes to bid him the last good-by.

The burial of a child calls forth no mournful thought. Convinced that they are angels, who go to heaven, the Brazilians, after having exposed the child dressed in white and crowned with roses, place it in a little pink or red coffin. This casket is placed across the two door curtains of a *sega* [*sege*] (a kind of *coupé*, driven by two horses by a postilion) painted red, and at each side of the carriage four or six men on horseback, in red liveries, and large burning tapers in their hand, accompany the body to the cemetery.

It is not in the customs of the country that the parents should follow the body. On all the routes of the procession, the Brazilian ladies throw roses to the little angel; it is very touching.

That which struck me rather oddly upon my arrival was to hear the soldiers, upon returning from the burial of one of their officers or comrades, play quadrilles and polkas on their instruments. This jovial manner of carrying the body to earth seemed to me full of originality. I asked the reason. I was told that it was in order not to sadden the soldiers too much and to get up again their courage.

A mournful thing, for example, is to see the Holy Sacrament carried through the town. The *padre*, carrying the Christ, is followed by two choir-boys, one of whom rings a little bell from minute to minute. Accordingly, as the Holy Sacrament passes, all the inhabitants prostrate their faces to the ground, and the majority, especially the little negroes, follow it with candles, and in singing the psalms of deliverance.

All these people, in uttering mournful cries, accompany the priest to the door of the dying one, whom fright must finish off more than once assuredly.

One ignores [does not know], in Brazil, what gallantry is. When [in France] the women are young, one tells it to them with exaggerations of praise, and one does not fear to call them goddesses, divinities, etc. When they are so no longer, it is told to them just the same. Now, for the Brazilians, every woman who is past thirty is an old woman, and they would not be afraid to say to her then, *"Està acabada!"* (You are played out!) It is not very amiable, as you see.

To begin from this moment, a woman no longer counts. Likewise, the Brazilian ladies when come to this age generally give up society. They do up their hair with negligence, no matter how, no longer go out in the world at all, and remain all day in their loose dressing-gowns, and without corsets.

When the father or mother of the family is spoken of, the children, and even the slaves of the house, designate them by the names of *a velha, o velho* (old woman, old man); and yet the respect for the father is carried to the highest point. The children kiss his hand in the morning and in the evening, and would not dare embrace him. They never address them in the second person. All this forms rather a curious mixture, which greatly surprises Europeans.

Although the Brazilian people are very intelligent, they still ignore [do not know] (or at least they did years ago) what conversation means; they read little. Philosophical questions interested them but little at this time, and they never stirred up the religious questions.

They are Catholic without questioning, go to Mass regularly, burn candles for all the saints in paradise, and believe all possible and probable miracles, which does not prevent its clergy from being dissolute enough, and that one does not constrain one's self from saying at Rio, "That mulatto is the son of Padre S——."

If one catches a fish of great price in the bay, one also knows beforehand that it will be bought by the convent of Sao Bento; for the monks of this convent are Benedictines, renowned through the city for their greediness. They give each year a large feast, when, it is said, more than one woman, on this day, disguised in man's clothes, enters the convent and passes a part of the night.

This was told me by a little monk who had renounced orders, and who had left Sao Bento by scaling the walls.

All this is told in a low voice, but, however, does not prevent the respect of the people for the good monks, and in general for all those who wear the gown or cassock. The *padres* and the *frades* [monks] do what they like, and exercise a large influence in the bosom of the family.

Music excepted, the other arts were not at all yet appreciated in Brazil during our stay; likewise, subjects of conversation were not abundant. Add to this a climate that debilitates, a heat which forces you to fan and sponge yourself constantly, and you will understand why one converses so little in Brazil.

I, who came from the artistic centre of Paris, and who had been accustomed to listen to the debating of all social, political, literary, and artistic questions in my father's drawing-room, was much surprised upon my arrival at Rio by this absolute lack of conversation. Having gone to pay a visit in a Brazilian family, *o dono da casa* (the head of the family) began by asking us, naturally, "*Come [Como] esta?*" (How do you do?) After this conventionality, we expected something more; nothing coming, there was a silence, which the head of the house broke by repeating, "*Entaõ a senhora passon bein [passou bem]?*" (Then madam has been well?) "Very well," I replied for a second time; and I tried to speak of the theatre and of the prima donna in fashion. After two brief replies, exchanged upon the subject, the conversation again dropped, and gave place to a silence of several minutes, which seeing, our host thought it well to again renew the subject by addressing to me for the third time the question, "*Ora tem passado bein?*" (Well, then, you have been well?) This time I could stand it no longer, and, laughter overtaking us, my husband and I were obliged to take leave.

We saw later, on different occasions, that the "*Come passon?*" (How do you do?) is the customary manner in the land of renewing conversation, which ordinarily so languishingly flags that calls are shortened.

The *senhor fazendeiro*, of whom I have already spoken, would come, when he was in town, to see us three or four times a week. He would enter in a grave manner, inquire the state of our health, seat himself directly in front of me, and would not breathe a word. As I had been godmother over one of his children, I naturally tried to put myself out to make some conversation during his first comings, but I would become so tired that I found it more amusing in the end not to say anything at all. He would come in therefore, seat himself, remain there an hour, and sometimes two, without speaking, then would rise suddenly, and go off like a bomb-shell.

If one does not talk, one dances, in revenge, with force in Brazil, which is surprising, with the excessive heat.

Custom requires that the partner, after the square dance or waltz, take the arm of his lady, promenade her about a little in the drawing-room, and then lead her to the buffet; after which he bows to her and goes to another. For jealous people, this custom is extraordinary enough, for it is there that the customary declarations are attempted; and another custom not less extraordinary is that the cavalier drinks in the glass of his lady.

The secret correspondence of lovers is frequently enough made by means of the *Jornal do Comercio* (now one has an idea of it by the correspondence of the *Figaro*). There, two pages at least are consecrated to phrases in the style of these:—

"I waited for you yesterday, and you did not come! He who is dying of love for you implores an answer to his letter."

"O virgin, I have read heaven in thine eyes!"

"Don't pass under my windows any more: you are watched," etc.

Sometimes it is very amusing to follow this correspondence. Very frequently one sees a whole drama unrolling itself. Then there are mistakes: one letter has been taken for another, and the action becomes complicated.

As to what regards the army, I ignore [do not know] what mode of recruiting is employed to form it, but during my sojourn in Brazil it was composed of little else than mulattoes and negroes, which seemed very strange to me; for it was to the sons of the slaves that was intrusted the care of guarding the country which had enslaved their fathers. Every *hidalgo's* son is a cadet by right, which is to say, officer.

Since the war,* which Brazil has sustained with much courage, and which has been crowned with success, I have been assured that there are many more whites among the soldiers, and that the law of recruiting has been revised. In the moment of war, each Brazilian who gave five or six of his slaves as soldiers was ennobled, and the slaves free,—free to be soldiers, and to be killed.

Nothing is funnier than a negro dressed as a soldier. He reminds one of the monkeys dressed as generals, which our organ-grinders conduct through the streets, obliging them to drill.

In point [on the subject] of stage at Rio Janeiro, there is only the Théâtre Lyrique, where Italian opera is given, and which swell society attends. The theatre is very beautiful. All the boxes are very much exposed, which allows one to see the toilet of a lady from head to foot. One only goes there in *décolleté* dress and in short sleeves, and once a year the Emperor and Empress attend the play in full robes: it is on the day of the opening of the House,—the Emperor all bedizened with gold,

---

*The War of the Triple Alliance or Paraguayan War (1864–1870) in which Brazil, Argentina, and Uruguay fought and finally defeated Paraguay— Ed.

with the imperial mantle, and the Empress with the diadem, the mantle of ermine, and all the crown diamonds.

The other theatre, called Sao Pedro, where are represented [performed] the French dramas and comedies translated into Portuguese, does not attract the best society. It has already been burned down twice. The first tragedian in the land, Joao Cætanos [Caetano] dos Santos, who really possessed great talent, had taken its direction, and had added the ballet to comedy. Since his death, the theatre has completely fallen.

There have not yet been, I think, more than one or two Brazilian works represented, which goes to prove, whatever may be written in different works upon Brazil, that the nations of South America are yet very backward, from an artistic stand-point. They have a few poets, however, the best of whom are, in my opinion, Gonzalves Dias,* and Malgalhaes.† It is grace, above all, which dominates in the character of their poetry. I give a few as patterns [samples] at the end of the volume. [See Appendix.] Many words, many pictures, a certain harmony, but little of thought and depth; besides, here is what is said, over the literature, by one of its own compatriots: "The first aspect of any literature whatever is the lyrical; and should the precocious pride of our youth suffer by it, the Brazilian literature finds itself but only on the border, hardly in its infancy as yet, in the lyrical phase, in short."

"A primeira phase de uma literatura qualquer è o lyrismo, e mal que pere [pese] ao orgulho precoce da nossa mocidade, a literatura Brazileira acha se ainda nos primeiros limbos, acha se na sua infancia, à penenas [penas], na phase do lyrismo, enfine [enfim].—Dr. Cætano Filgueiras [Figueiras]."

This is judging the question well. One of their best novels has for its title *Le* [*O*] *Guarany*, by Alaincar [José de Alencar], and of which I propose to offer a translation one of these days

*Antonio Gonçalves Dias (1823–1864)—Ed.
†Domingos José Gonçalves de Magalhães (1811–1882)—Ed.

to the Parisian public. It is a faithful painting of the life of the Indian, which is at the same time poetical and true. I have also translated from the Brazilian a little novel, called *Cinco Minutos*, which is not lacking in originality; it is also by the pen of d'Alaincar, whose talent is incontestable.

The Brazilian language, with all its diminutives of *zinha*, *zinhos*, has an entire creole grace, and I never can hear it spoken without finding a great charm in it: it is the Portuguese with its nasal accent modified. The mother tongue has evidently degenerated. "It is a kind of *patois*," say the Portuguese. Never mind: all its caressing endings are becoming to it, and give to the Brazilian tongue a "something" which captivates the ear far more than the pure language of Camoéns.*

The Eldorado, *café chantant* (café), which was opened at Rio Janeiro some fifteen years ago, has brought our popular operettas into fashion over there, and the stars of this theatre return from there loaded with diamonds. It is at the Eldorado that the Brazilian youths go and take their French lesson every evening: judge, therefore.

When one wishes to make the journey to Brazil, the best season to accomplish it is in May or June, because then you arrive in winter, and have a better chance to become acclimated, and avoiding yellow fever, which, besides, is no longer as deadly, and which, in taking precautions, one can guard against. Moreover, the trips across at this time of the year are delightful.

When I returned to Brazil for the second time, after a year's stay in my own country, I did not wish to take to the sea before the month of May; likewise, the voyage was a perfect promenade.

I had embarked on a magnificent clipper, called the "Paulista," Capt. Callange.

---

*Luis Vaz de Camoëns (c.1524–1580), the great epic poet of Portugal, author of *Os Lusíadas (The Lusiads)*—Ed.

One day while I was on deck, a superb Newfoundland dog, with a long and glossy coat, intelligent and kind eyes, approached me, and began lapping the hands of my child, seated on my knees. I caressed him, and asked to whom he belonged.

"He is mine," said the captain; "and I am so attached to him that, on my last voyage, as Pollux (the dog's name) had taken a notion to jump overboard to take a sea-bath at the moment when we were having a splendid breeze and running twenty-five knots an hour, at the risk of breaking masts and rudder, I ordered the pilot to immediately turn the helm to the wind, to allow the dog to rejoin us; and I can assure you there wasn't a murmur in the crew for this manœuvre, which had in view, after all, but an animal's life."

"He is then much beloved by the sailors?"

"It is but just. Think of it: they owe to him the life of one of their own. Three years ago, we were at the entrance of the British Channel, always so bad; the wind was blowing from the east, a tempest was coming. I commanded one of my men to tackle the sails, and one of them, in executing this order, fell into the water. At this cry of, 'A man has fallen into the sea!' I hastened, in spite of the dreadful weather we were having, to stop the clipper's run, and the sailors hastened to throw from all sides salvage buoys to their unfortunate comrade.

"Pollux, at the cry given by the crew, had immediately jumped into the waves, in search of the sailor, who, not knowing how to swim (for it is incredible how many there are in this case), did not reappear. The brave dog dived and dived in again. Soon we saw him reappear, holding the man by his cravat; but at the moment when he appeared on the water's surface the cravat gave way, and the unfortunate man disappeared for a second time. The distress of the poor dog is extreme; he tries in vain to seize the sailor by the hair, whose head, close shaven, offers no hold. There we were, breathless, watching the turns of this rescue. Finally, we see Pollux holding the man by his shirt, and struggling thus some moments against the waves; then, seeing that the sailor is debilitated, and almost without consciousness, the intelligent animal then glides under him, lifts him up, and swims thus in holding his head above water, which allows the poor devil to regain his consciousness. From time to time Pollux also reappears, to take a breath in his turn, then hastens to regain his post under the man, whom he finally brings next to the ship, where, fresh ropes having been thrown to him, the poor sailor could be taken on board, thanks to my brave dog, who himself had much pain to remount, and fell upon the deck exhausted with fatigue.

"Then, not knowing how to be grateful enough for the devotion and the courage of Pollux, the crew decreed, all present, and unanimously, that such an animal should be treated as a man; that henceforth his ration should be previously [first] levied from that of the sailors, and that he should have his place reserved in their midst at meal hours. If you care to be present at noon, in the back of the ship, madam, you can assure yourself of the veracity of my story."

I did not allow him to tell me twice, and at the sailors' dinner hour I was present at a curious sight.

The whole crew were ranged in a circle, and each one, spoon in hand, was waiting his turn to dip into the immense porringer, against which a smaller one had been placed; this one belonged to Pollux, that, with the first stroke of the bell, ran up to take his accustomed place in the midst of his friends, of whom he each day learned some new trick. The brave dog then sat down to eat his soup, with all the dignity which his new social position required, only wagging his tail in a sign of joy each time that one of the sailors would pronounce his name.

So here is the very true history of the dog of the "Paulista."

Therefore, to return to voyages of South America: one must never undertake them in September or March.

I had the imprudence to sail once in this last-named month, and besides the cold I endured, which almost made me ill, we were exposed to such a tempest that I thought I should never see France again.

It was one o'clock in the morning; all were sleeping on board excepting the officers on duty, when suddenly we were awakened by a dreadful crash. It seemed to us as if the ship were smashing itself to pieces, and water filled our cabins. I heard screaming from all sides: "We are sinking, captain! Help! Help!" I took my child in my arms, and stayed with him in the highest berth, waiting with anxiety for what would happen next.

There was, during half an hour, an infernal noise on deck; there was a jumping; the reefs of the sails were taken in; sails were taken to roof the saloon, whose roof had been swept away; there was a going up and a coming down; orders followed each other; and the ship, tossed by the tempest, threw our poor bodies against the partitions of the cabins, soon to the right, soon to the left, without giving us a moment's intermission. At last, the uproar seemed to calm itself a little on deck, and the captain entered my cabin, in saying, "Now, then! are we dead here?" I asked him what had happened. He answered me that we were at the entrance of the British Channel, that a terrible tempest had suddenly arisen, and that an enormous wave having come under the ship had swept over the deck, carrying away with it the roof of the saloon, sweeping away hen-coops, benches, etc., everything which was on deck still, and even breaking a mast. "There is little water in the hold of the ship, fortunately," he added, "but we could not stand another wave like this."

I arose with much pain, the pitching being frightful, and sought refuge with my son in one of the cabins where the water had not entered; then I wished to go on deck, to contemplate the spectacle of the sea in its fury. I could risk myself no farther than the last steps of the saloon stair, clinging with all force to the balustrade, and what I then beheld will never be effaced from my memory.

Immense waves, resembling high mountains, surrounded our ship on all sides, and lifted it to their height, only to let it drop into the abyss. One could not conceive of a passage being made in the midst of these mountains of foaming water, which threatened to engulf it at each moment. I quickly descended, completely horrified, and the majority of the men on deck did as I did. Hardly had they tried to contemplate this spectacle than one saw them returning, pale and mute.

Cooking could no longer be done. Twice had the soup been spilled on deck by the cabin-boy who brought it; one had to be satisfied with preserves and cold victuals.

This terrible tempest lasted three days, during which no one took a breath; one could do nothing: one waited. At the end of the second day we took on the pilot, who had much trouble to embark, and told us on arriving, "You are very lucky to have got off at so little cost. The whole channel is strewn with shipwrecks." At last the wind fell, and we could enter Havre, where, after having landed, I vowed to myself that nevermore should the month of March see me on the ocean.

With what happiness I again saw France, after ten years passed in America! I remember my joy at the sight of a bouquet of lilacs. "Some lilacs!" said I, with tears in my eyes; "some lilacs! It is such a long time since I have seen any." The proprietress of the hotel, who had heard me, had a bouquet sent me to my room.

However, many were the astonishments and disillusions which awaited me upon returning. My country, which had remained so beautiful in my memory, seemed to me barren, sad, dull, in comparison to the one I had just left. When I perceived from the window of the car our fields cut up into little squares of all shades, it gave me the effect of a hearth-rug whose squares had been sewn one to another. Our parks reminded me of the sheepfolds given children on New-Year's day. Far from being enraptured (as I ought perhaps to have been) over the cultivation of this land, of which the smallest corner is sown full, and produces, it shocked me, and appeared to me of an unheard-of meanness. This land, where not an inch of ground was lost, where nothing was given, where the smallest bit of ground was bought, closed my heart up, in spite of myself. I recalled to myself those long miles travelled over in Brazil, where nature alone takes care to bear the costs, where the unhappy one could pluck at his leisure a banana, an orange, and the palmetto without being disturbed by whomsoever it might be, drink water fresh from the spring without its being sold to him, sleep in the forest without a policeman's arresting him.

Under our narrow civilization, it was with pains that I could again find nature the same, as I have often looked hard to see the sky, which the tall houses of our cities conceal from our view.

How many the times that I have regretted those immense horizons, which elevate the soul and the thoughts, my sea-baths in the moonlight on the phosphorescent beach, my horse-back rides through the mountains, that beautiful bay on which the windows of my house looked out, and where, at night, the boats of the fishermen would pass, bearing their torches over the waves.

Accustomed to occupy a large house, where I could offer hospitality to eight people, without incommoding myself, I had hard work to accustom myself anew to our Parisian life, so narrow, so luxuriant in appearance, and so scrimped in its reality, where each morsel is counted at our tables, where you look [think twice] before changing your linen daily, where the very air seems measured. " 'Tis, however, in the rich countries, I was told that all that is produced. I will admit it; but I prefer then those that are called poor where living is large, where the air and the sun are not meted out to you, where single fruit is not divided in four, where one bathes every day, and where, for almost nothing, one can buy, not simply a small corner of ground, but miles of land.

One thing consoled me upon my return for the littleness of material existence. "Here I am, returned to the country of thought and progress," said I.

Alas! I found everything much changed. The Parisians no longer conversed: they smoked, and spoke a kind of impossible cant. I fell back upon the theatres: comic operas alone were fashionable. The sillier it was, the more my compatriots would laugh. There always had to be at a certain given moment of the play five or six personages [characters] who would come to the centre of action dancing a kind of crazy can-can, and the public would pleasurably burst with laughter.

Where had the Gallic mind gone to? where had the language of the eighteenth century gone to? where had the gallantry and the elegant conversations of our fathers gone to? I asked myself.

Was it then I who saw false, or the people of my country? That was the question I frequently set to myself with uneasiness.

Whatever it may be, I acquired the conviction that when one has lived in those countries bathed in sunshine, one can no more live anywhere else; and that when the soul has strongly steeped itself in the sight of the grand works of God, it can no longer understand the artificial life of our cities.

This is what makes me always *saudade* (homesick), as the Brazilians say, for South America, and that I long to see it once again before I die.

Appendix*

―⊰❦⊱―

Cauçao do Exílio

Minha terra tem palmeiras
Onde canta o Sabiá;
As aves que aqui gorgeião,
Não gorgeião como lá.

Nosso ceo tem mais estrellas,
Nossos varzeas tem mais flores,
Nossos bosques tem mais vida,
Nossa vida mais amores.

Em scismar, sosinho, à noite,
Mais prazer encontro eu lá.
Minha terra tem palmeiras
Onde canta o Sabiá.

Minha terra tem primores,
Que taes não encontro eu cá
Em scismar, sosinho—à noite—
Mais prazer encontro eu lá.
Minha terra tem palmeiras
Onde canta o Sabiá.

*These poems are here given first in the original, then the French trans-
lation, and lastly, the English.

103

Não permita Deos que eu morra
Sem que eu volte para lá
Sem que desfructe os primores
Que não encontro por cá,
Sem qu'inda aviste as palmeiras
Onde canta o Sabiá.

—◦⦿◦—

Chant de L'exil

Mon pays a des ombrages
Où chante le Sabiá.
Les oiseaux de vos parages
Ne chantent pas comme là.

Notre ciel a plus d'étoiles,
Nos compagnes plus de fleurs,
Nos bois vivants plus de voiles,
Plus d'amour aussi nos cœurs.

A rêver seul, sur tes plages,
Quel plaisir j'ai goûté là!
Ses palmiers ont des ombrages
Où chante le Sabiá.

Seul, la nuit, sur ton rivage,
Serre du magnolia!
Aux doux parfums de ta plage,
Quels doux rêves j'ai fait là!
Mon pays a des ombrages
Où chante le Sabiá.

Ne permets pas que je meure,
O Dieu! sans revenir là,

Revoir, à ma dernière heure,
La fleur de Maracaja,
Et mes palmiers que je pleure,
Où chante le Sabiá.*

⟨⟩

Song of Exile

My country has shades
Where the Sabiá† sings.
The bird of your glades
No like melody brings.

Our heaven has more stars,
Our fields have more flowers,
Our woods have more life,
Our life has more love.

Dreaming by the sea-waves
Unforgotten pleasure brings,
In thy palm-trees' shades,
Where the Sabiá sings.

Alone, at night, on the shore
Of thy magnolia land,
Perfumed breezes wafted o'er
My dreams, so sweetly made
In the palm-trees' shade,
Where the Sabiá sings.

*This Brazilian poetry, of [Antonio] Gonçalves Dias, which has been set to music by M. Amat, accompanied by the guitar, has an exquisite grace and the perfume of the country. I have had the pleasure of having it heard at my home sometimes, and, thanks to the composer, it always was the success of the evening.
†Song thrush—Ed.

Permit not that I should die,
O God, without returning
There, to see in my last hour
The magnolia flower,
And my palms, for whom I sigh,
With the Sabiá's singing.

———

O Escravo!

POR LUIZ FAGUNDES VARELLA

Dorme! benidito o archanjo tenebroso
Cujo dedo immortal
Gravou-a te sobre a testa bronzeado
O sigillo fatal!
Dorme! se a terra devorou sedenta
De teu rosto o suor
Mai compassiva agora te agasalha
Com zelo e com amor.

Ninguem te disse o adeus da despedida
Ninguem por ti chorou
Embora! A humanidade em teu sudario
Os olhos euxugou!
A verdade luzio por um momento
De teus irmãos à grei
Se vivo, foste escravo, es morto—livre
Pela suprema lei!

Tu suspiraste como o Hebreu captivo
Saudoso do Jordão
Pesado achaste o ferro da revolta
Não o quizeste, não!

Lançaste-o sobre a terra inconsciente
De teu proprio poder
Contra o direito, contra a natureza
Preferiste morrer!

Do augusto condemnado as leis são santas
São leis porém de amor
Por amor de ti mesmo e dos mais homens
Precisa era o valor.
Não o tiveste! os ferros e os açoites
Mattarão-te a razaõ
Dobrado captivero! a teus algozes
Dobrada punição.

Porque nos teus momente de supplicio
De agonia e de dor.
Não chamaste das terras Africanas
O vento assolador?
Elle traria a força e a persistencia
A tu'alma sem fé.
Nos rugidos dos tigres de Benguella
Dos leões de Guiné!

Elle traria o fogo dos desertos
O sol dos areaes
A voz de teus irmãos viril et forte
O brado de teus pais!
Elle te sopraria às molles fibras
A raiva do suão.
Quando agitando as crinas inflammadas
Fustiga a solidão.

Então ergueras resoluto a fronte
E grande em teu valor
Mostraras que em teu seio inda vibrava
A voz do Creador.

Mostraras que das sombras do martyrio
Tambem rebenta a luz
Oh! teus grilhões serião tão sublimes
Tão santos como a cruz!

Mas morreste sem luctas, sem protestos,
Sem um grito sequer
Como a ovelha no altar, como a criança
No ventre da mulher.
Morreste sem mostrar que tinhas n'alma
Uma chispa do Cèo
Como se um crime sobre ti pesasse
Como se fóras réo!

Sem defeza sem preces sem lamentos.
Sem cyrios, sem caixão
Passaste da senzala ao cemitério
Do lixo à podridão!
Sua essencia immortal onde é que estava?
Onde as leis do Senhor?
Digão-no o tronco, o latego, as algemas
E as ordens de feitor!

Eras o mesmo ser, a mesma essencia
Que teu bárbaro algoz
Forão seus dias de rosada seda
Os teus, de atro retroz.
Patria, familia, ideas, esperanças,
Crenças, religião,
Tudo matou-te, em flor no intimo d'alma
O dedo da oppressão.

Tudo, tudo abateu sem do nem pena
Tudo, tudo, meu Deos!

E teu olhar à lama condemnado
Esqueceu-se dos Céos!
Dorme! bendito o Archanjo tenebroso
Cuja cifra immortal
Sellando-te o sepulero, abrio-te os olhos
A' luz universal!

L'Esclave

POÉSIE DE FAGUNDES VARELLA

Dors! Béni soit l'archange des ténèbres,
Dont le doigt immortel
A gravé sur ta tête bronzée
Le sceau fatal!
Dors! Si la terre altérée
A bu la sueur de ton front,
Mère compatissante, à présente elle t'enveloppe
Avec soin et amour.

Personne ne t'a dit l'adieu suprême,
Personne n'a pleuré sur toi.
Qu'importe! L'humanité à ton suaire
S'est essuyé les yeux.
La vérité a lui pour un moment
Sur le sort de tes frères.
Si, vivant, tu fus esclave, tu es mort libre
De par la loi suprême.

Tu soupirais comme l'Hébreu captif
Regrettant le Jourdain;
Mais tu ne voulus pas t'armer pour la révolte,
Tu ne voulus pas, non!

Tu passas sur la terre, inconscient
De ton propre pouvoir.
Contre ton droit, et malgré la nature,
Tu préféras mourir.

Du divin condamné pourtant les lois sont saintes,
Et ces lois sont toutes d'amour.
Pour l'amour de toi-même et pour l'amour des autres,
Il te fallait prendre courage.
Tu n'en eus pas! La prison et le fouet
Ont tué ta raison.
Double captivité! Pour tes bourreaux aussi,
Châtiment double.

Pourquoi, dans tes moments de supplice,
De douleur, d'agonie,
N'appelais-tu pas, de l'Afrique,
Le vent dévastateur?
Il aurait apporté force et persévérance
A ton âme sans foi,
Dans les rugissements des tigres du Bengale
Et des lions de Guinée!

Il t'aurait apporté le feu de tes déserts
Et le soleil ardent des sables,
Et la voix de tes frères, forte et virile,
Et le cri de tes pères.
Il aurait soufflé sur tes fibres amollies
La rage du simoun,
Lorsque, agitant ses crinières enflammées,
Il fustige le désert.

Alors, tu aurais relevé la tête fièrement,
Et, grand dans ton courage,
Tu aurais prouvé que dans ton âme
Vibrait encore la voix du Créateur,

Et que, des ombres du martyre,
Peut aussi jaillir la lumière.
Oh! tes chaînes, alors, eussent pu être belles,
Et sainte aussi ta croix!

Sans protestations, sans lutte tu mourus,
Sans même un cri,
Comme la brebis sur l'autel,
Comme l'enfant dans le sein maternel.
To mourus sans montrer que tu portais dans l'âme
Une etincelle encore du ciel,
Comme si quelque crime, enfin, pesait sur toi,
Et que tu te sentisses coupable.

Sans defense, sans prières, sans lamentations,
San cierges, sans même une bière,
Tu as passé de la senzala au cimetière,
De la boue à la pourriture.
Où donc était ton essence immortelle
Et la loi du Seigneur?
En prison, sous le fouet, on sous de lourdes chaines,
Aux ordres du feitor.

Tu étais cependant un être de la même essence
Que ton barbare bourreau.
Pourquoi ses jours furent-ils tissés de soie rose
Et les tiens tissés de noir?
Et Patrie, et famille, esperances, pensée.
Saintes croyances, religion,
Tout mouruten sa fleur, dans le fond de ton âme,
Sous le joug de l' oppression.

Tout, elle abattit tout, sans remords et sans peine,
Tout, hélas! tout, mon Dieu!
Et ton ceil, condamné pour jamais à la boue,
Fut oublieux du ciel.

Dors! Beni soit l'archange des tenèbres
Dont la main immortelle,
En te scellant dans le sépulcre, ouvrit tes yeux
A la lumiere éternelle.

The Slave

POETRY BY FAGUNDES VARELLA
(CALLED THE BRAZILIAN MUSSET)

Sleep! Blessed be the archangel of darkness,
Whose immortal finger
Hath graven on thy bronzed head
The fatal seal!
Sleep! If the thirsty world
Hath drunk the sweat of thy brow,
Compassionate Mother Earth now envelops thee
With care and love.

No one bade thee a last good-by,
No tear was shed o'er thee—
Who cares? Humanity at thy shroud
Hath wiped its eyes.
Truth shone for a moment
O'er the fate of thy brethren.
If living, thou wast in bonds, dying thou becamest free
By the law divine.

Thou wast sighing like captive Israel
Regretting Jordan;
But thou wouldst not arm thyself for conflict,—
Thou wouldst not, no!
Thou didst pass o'er the earth unconscious
Of thy rightful power

'Gainst thy right, 'gainst nature,
Thou preferredst death.

Yet the divine Condemned One's laws are holy,
And those laws are full of love,
For love of self and for love of others.
Thou shouldst have taken courage.
Thou hadst not : prison bars and lash
Had killed thy reason.
Double captivity! For thy oppressors too
Double chastisement.

Why, in thy moments of torment,
Pain, and agony,
Calledst thou not Africa's
Devastating wind?
It would have brought strength and perseverance
To thy fainting soul,
In the roaring of the tigers of Bengal
And the lions of Guinea.

It would have brought thee the fire of thy deserts
And the burning sun o'er the sands,
And the voice of thy brethren, strong and manly,
With the cry of thy fathers.
It would have blown on thy bruised limbs
Simuom's* fury,
When, shaking his enfuriated manes,
He sweeps the desert.

Then, lifting thy head proudly,
And strong in thy courage,
Thou wouldst have proven that in thy soul
Vibrated still the Creator's voice,

*A searing desert wind—Ed.

And that out of the shades of martyrdom
Light can burst.
Oh! then could thy chains have been glorious,
And sacred also thy cross!

Without struggling, without protestations,
Not even a cry, thou didst die
Like the lamb upon the altar,
Even as the unborn child.
Thou didst die without showing that in thy soul
Still smouldered a spark of heaven,
As if some crime still weighed upon thee
And by its guilt accused thee.

Without defense, without prayer, without tears,
Without tapers, not even a bier,
Thou didst pass from the hut to the grave,
From mire to decay.
Where then was thine immortal soul,
And the Saviour's law?
In prison, under the lash, or in heavy chains
Under the oppressor's command.

Yet thou wast a being of the same essence
As thy barbarous oppressor,
Why were his days woven in rose-color
And thine in black?
Father-land and family, hopes, thoughts,
Holy creeds, religion,
All died in their prime, in the depth of thy soul,
Under the oppressor's yoke.

All, all was crushed, without remorse or feeling,
All, alas! all, my God!

And thine eye, evermore condemned to the earth,
Lost sight of heaven.
Sleep! Blessed be the archangel of darkness,
Whose immortal hand
In sealing thy sepulchre opened thine eyes
To eternal light.

Bibliographical Essay

June E. Hahner

The nineteenth century was the period of peak popularity for travel literature. Among the Latin American countries, Brazil and Mexico received the most attention from travel writers. Those who came to Rio de Janeiro are listed in Paulo Berger, *Bibliografia do Rio de Janeiro de viajantes e autores estangeiros, 1531–1900* (Rio de Janeiro: Livraria São José, 1964). French accounts of Brazil, not as numerous as those written by travelers from Great Britain or the United States, are noted in Gilda Maria Whitaker Verri, *Viajantes franceses no Brasil. Bibliografia* (Recife: Editora Universitária UFPE, 1994). Maria Dundas Graham (Lady Callcott) wrote the best-known travel account by a woman about Brazil, one long appreciated for its accuracy and strengths of observation: *Journal of a Voyage to Brazil, and Residence There, During Part of the Years 1821, 1822, 1823* (London: Longman, Hurst, Rees, Orme, Brown, and Green, 1824). One of the most popular accounts in the nineteenth century, and one often cited since then, is that by two Protestant missionaries, James C. Fletcher and Daniel Paris Kidder, *Brazil and the Brazilians Portrayed in Historical and Descriptive Sketches*, 7th ed. (Boston: Little, Brown, 1867), which includes comments on Brazilian women and families. A young German school teacher, Ina von Binzer, who worked as a governess and teacher in Brazil in the early 1880s, published a unique series of letters which tell us much about home life among the elite: *Alegrias e tristezas de uma educadora alemã no Brasil*, trans. Alice Rossi and Luisita da Gama Cerqueira (São Paulo: Editora Anhembi, 1956).

Travel literature itself has long served as a subject of interest for writers and scholars, who have written far more about travelers to other parts of the world than about those who visited Latin America. Selections focusing on Latin American women drawn from accounts by nineteenth-century female visitors to the region are found in June E. Hahner, ed., *Women through Women's Eyes: Latin American Women in Nineteenth-Century Travel Accounts* (Wilmington, DE: Scholarly Resources, 1998). Several dozen excerpts from accounts by foreign travelers, mostly male, that deal with women and their activities in nineteenth-century Rio de Janeiro are collected in Miriam Moreira Leite, ed., *A condição feminina no Rio de Janeiro. Século XIX. Antologia de textos de viajantes estrangeiros* (São Paulo and Brasília: Editora Hucitec/Instituto Nacional do Livro, 1984). Her *Livros de Viagem (1803/1900)* (Rio de Janeiro: Editora UFRJ, 1997) contains articles on nineteenth-century travel literature that were written during the many years she spent studying this subject.

In recent years the development of colonial discourse analysis has focused new attention on travel writing, often seen as one of the intellectual supports of empire, and scholars have combined ideological and cultural critiques with studies in genre. Latin America is included in Mary Louise Pratt's excellent study, *Imperial Eyes: Travel Writing and Transculturation* (London: Routledge, 1992). Sara Mills sets British travelers within the colonial context and discourse, using Michel Foucault's work as the frame for *Differences of Discourse: An Analysis of Women's Travel Writings and Colonialism* (London: Routledge, 1991).

The newest general histories of Brazil in English are those by Boris Fausto, *A Concise History of Brazil*, trans.

Arthur Brakel (New York: Cambridge University Press, 1999), and Thomas E. Skidmore, *Brazil: Five Centuries of Change* (New York and Oxford: Oxford University Press, 1999). A solid text, long employed in classrooms, which has gone through several revised editions, is E. Bradford Burns, *A History of Brazil*, 3d ed. (New York: Columbia University Press, 1993). The centrality of Emperor Pedro II to Brazil's nineteenth-century political history becomes apparent from a new biography based on meticulous scholarship by Roderick J. Barman, *Citizen Emperor: Pedro II and the Making of Brazil, 1825–91* (Stanford: Stanford University Press, 1999). The essays of Emilia Viotti da Costa collected in *The Brazilian Empire: Myths and Histories*, rev. ed. (Chapel Hill and London: University of North Carolina Press, 2000), treat important aspects of the history of the empire.

African slavery, a fundamental factor in Brazil's history, provided the foundation for the country's export-oriented economy during most of the nineteenth century. Gilberto Freyre's classic work on slavery and plantation life in northeastern Brazil, *The Masters and the Slaves*, trans. Samuel Putnam (New York: Alfred A. Knopf, 1946), although long subject to criticism and revisionism, still provides rewarding reading. A newer classic, Stanley J. Stein's *Vassouras: A Brazilian Coffee County, 1850–1890* (Cambridge, MA: Harvard University Press, 1957), provides us with a model monograph on the plantation economy and society, as does Warren Dean, *Rio Claro: A Brazilian Plantation System, 1820–1920* (Stanford: Stanford University Press, 1976). Stuart B. Schwartz's massive study, *Sugar Plantations in the Formation of Brazilian Society: Bahía, 1550–1835* (New York: Cambridge University Press, 1985), goes into all aspects of Bahía's sugar industry from its inception until the 1830s. In *To Be a Slave in Brazil, 1550–1888*, trans. Arthur Goldhammer (New

Brunswick, NJ: Rutgers University Press, 1986), Kátia M. de Queirós Mattoso traces slavery in Brazil over a three-hundred-year period, focusing on the slaves themselves. Mary Karasch's detailed, well-documented, and clearly organized study, *Slave Life in Rio de Janeiro, 1808–1850* (Princeton: Princeton University Press, 1987), focuses on slave life in the capital during the period when the slave presence there was at its height, while Sidney Chalhoub, *Visões da liberdade. Uma história das últimas décadas da escravidão na Corte* (São Paulo: Companhia das Letras, 1990), treats slavery in Rio during a later period. The documents collected by Robert Edgar Conrad, *Children of God's Fire: A Documentary History of Black Slavery in Brazil* (Princeton: Princeton University Press, 1983), provide a vivid record of slavery and the slave system, with its suffering and human exploitation. The abolition of slavery in Brazil is the focus of studies by Robert Edgar Conrad, *The Destruction of Brazilian Slavery, 1850–1888* (Berkeley: University of California Press, 1972), and Brent Toplin, *The Abolition of Slavery in Brazil* (New York: Atheneum, 1975).

Although the number of studies on women in nineteenth-century Brazil is still quite limited as compared to those on twentieth-century women, this scholarship continues to increase. The activities of poor women are documented in the studies by Maria Odila Leite da Silva Dias, *Power and Everyday Life: The Lives of Working Women in Nineteenth-Century Brazil*, trans. Ann Frost (New Brunswick, NJ: Rutgers University Press, 1995), and Sandra Lauderdale Graham, *House and Street: The Domestic World of Servants and Masters in Nineteenth-Century Rio de Janeiro* (Cambridge: Cambridge University Press, 1988). The dowry, one of the legal mechanisms that created and consolidated women's status, is the focus of the longitudinal study by Muriel Nazarri, *Disappearance of the Dowry: Women, Families, and Social Change in São Paulo, Brazil, 1600–1900* (Stanford: Stanford University Press, 1991). In *Emancipating the Female Sex: The Struggle for Women's Rights in Brazil, 1850–1940* (Durham, NC: Duke University Press, 1990), June E. Hahner traces the struggle for women's rights in Brazil from its earliest manifestations in the midnineteenth century. The studies by Kátia M. de Queirós Mattoso, *Família e sociedade na Bahía do século XIX* (São Paulo: Corrupio, 1988), Eni de Mesquita Samara, *As mulheres e o poder e a família. São Paulo, século XIX* (São Paulo: Marco Zero, 1989), and Dain Borges, *The Family in Bahía, Brazil, 1870–1940* (Stanford: Stanford University Press, 1992), extend well beyond elite families. An extensive bibliography of works on women in Brazil can be found in June E. Hahner, *Women in Brazil* (Albuquerque: Latin American Institute, University of New Mexico Press, 1998).

Latin American Silhouettes
Studies in History and Culture

William H. Beezley and
Judith Ewell
Editors

Volumes Published

Brian Loveman and Thomas M. Davies, Jr., eds., *The Politics of Antipolitics: The Military in Latin America*, 3d ed., revised and updated (1996).
Cloth ISBN 0-8420-2609-6
Paper ISBN 0-8420-2611-8

Dianne Walta Hart, *Undocumented in L.A.: An Immigrant's Story* (1997).
Cloth ISBN 0-8420-2648-7
Paper ISBN 0-8420-2649-5

William H. Beezley and Judith Ewell, eds., *The Human Tradition in Modern Latin America* (1997). Cloth ISBN 0-8420-2612-6   Paper ISBN 0-8420-2613-4

Donald F. Stevens, ed., *Based on a True Story: Latin American History at the Movies* (1997).
Cloth ISBN 0-8420-2582-0
Paper ISBN 0-8420-2781-5

Jaime E. Rodríguez O., ed., *The Origins of Mexican National Politics, 1808–1847* (1997). Paper ISBN 0-8420-2723-8

Che Guevara, *Guerrilla Warfare*, with revised and updated introduction and case studies by Brian Loveman and Thomas M. Davies, Jr., 3d ed. (1997). Cloth ISBN 0-8420-2677-0   Paper ISBN 0-8420-2678-9

Adrian A. Bantjes, *As If Jesus Walked on Earth: Cardenismo, Sonora, and the Mexican Revolution* (1998; rev. ed., 2000). Cloth ISBN 0-8420-2653-3
Paper ISBN 0-8420-2751-3

A. Kim Clark, *The Redemptive Work: Railway and Nation in Ecuador, 1895–1930* (1998). Cloth ISBN 0-8420-2674-6
Paper ISBN 0-8420-5013-2

Louis A. Pérez, Jr., ed., *Impressions of Cuba in the Nineteenth Century: The Travel Diary of Joseph J. Dimock* (1998).
Cloth ISBN 0-8420-2657-6
Paper ISBN 0-8420-2658-4

June E. Hahner, ed., *Women through Women's Eyes: Latin American Women in Nineteenth-Century Travel Accounts* (1998). Cloth ISBN 0-8420-2633-9
Paper ISBN 0-8420-2634-7

James P. Brennan, ed., *Peronism and Argentina* (1998). ISBN 0-8420-2706-8

John Mason Hart, ed., *Border Crossings: Mexican and Mexican-American Workers* (1998). Cloth ISBN 0-8420-2716-5
Paper ISBN 0-8420-2717-3

Brian Loveman, *For* la Patria: *Politics and the Armed Forces in Latin America* (1999). Cloth ISBN 0-8420-2772-6 Paper ISBN 0-8420-2773-4

Guy P. C. Thomson, with David G. LaFrance, *Patriotism, Politics, and Popular Liberalism in Nineteenth-Century Mexico: Juan Francisco Lucas and the Puebla Sierra* (1999).
ISBN 0-8420-2683-5

Robert Woodmansee Herr, in collaboration with Richard Herr, *An American Family in the Mexican Revolution* (1999).
ISBN 0-8420-2724-6

Juan Pedro Viqueira Albán, trans. Sonya Lipsett-Rivera and Sergio Rivera Ayala, *Propriety and Permissiveness in Bourbon Mexico* (1999).
Cloth ISBN 0-8420-2466-2
Paper ISBN 0-8420-2467-0

Stephen R. Niblo, *Mexico in the 1940s: Modernity, Politics, and Corruption* (1999).
Cloth ISBN 0-8420-2794-7
Paper (2001) ISBN 0-8420-2795-5

David E. Lorey, *The U.S.-Mexican Border in the Twentieth Century* (1999).
Cloth ISBN 0-8420-2755-6
Paper ISBN 0-8420-2756-4

Joanne Hershfield and David R. Maciel, eds., *Mexico's Cinema: A Century of Films and Filmmakers* (2000). Cloth ISBN 0-8420-2681-9 Paper ISBN 0-8420-2682-7

Peter V. N. Henderson, *In the Absence of Don Porfirio: Francisco León de la Barra*

and the Mexican Revolution (2000).
ISBN 0-8420-2774-2

Mark T. Gilderhus, *The Second Century: U.S.-Latin American Relations since 1889* (2000). Cloth ISBN 0-8420-2413-1 Paper ISBN 0-8420-2414-X

Catherine Moses, *Real Life in Castro's Cuba* (2000). Cloth ISBN 0-8420-2836-6 Paper ISBN 0-8420-2837-4

K. Lynn Stoner, ed./comp., with Luis Hipólito Serrano Pérez, *Cuban and Cuban-American Women: An Annotated Bibliography* (2000). ISBN 0-8420-2643-6

Thomas D. Schoonover, *The French in Central America: Culture and Commerce, 1820–1930* (2000). ISBN 0-8420-2792-0

Enrique C. Ochoa, *Feeding Mexico: The Political Uses of Food since 1910* (2000). ISBN 0-8420-2812-9

Thomas W. Walker and Ariel C. Armony, eds., *Repression, Resistance, and Democratic Transition in Central America* (2000). Cloth ISBN 0-8420-2766-1 Paper ISBN 0-8420-2768-8

William H. Beezley and David E. Lorey, eds., *¡Viva México! ¡Viva la Independencia! Celebrations of September 16* (2001). Cloth ISBN 0-8420-2914-1 Paper ISBN 0-8420-2915-X

Jeffrey M. Pilcher, *Cantinflas and the Chaos of Mexican Modernity* (2001). Cloth ISBN 0-8420-2769-6 Paper ISBN 0-8420-2771-8

Victor M. Uribe-Uran, ed., *State and Society in Spanish America during the Age of Revolution* (2001). Cloth ISBN 0-8420-2873-0 Paper ISBN 0-8420-2874-9

Andrew Grant Wood, *Revolution in the Street: Women, Workers, and Urban*

Protest in Veracruz, 1870–1927 (2001). ISBN 0-8420-2879-X

Charles Bergquist, Ricardo Peñaranda, and Gonzalo Sánchez G., eds., *Violence in Colombia, 1990–2000: Waging War and Negotiating Peace* (2001). Cloth ISBN 0-8420-2869-2 Paper ISBN 0-8420-2870-6

William Schell, Jr., *Integral Outsiders: The American Colony in Mexico City, 1876–1911* (2001). ISBN 0-8420-2838-2

John Lynch, *Argentine Caudillo: Juan Manuel de Rosas* (2001). Cloth ISBN 0-8420-2897-8 Paper ISBN 0-8420-2898-6

Samuel Basch, M.D., ed. and trans. Fred D. Ullman, *Recollections of Mexico: The Last Ten Months of Maximilian's Empire* (2001). ISBN 0-8420-2962-1

David Sowell, *The Tale of Healer Miguel Perdomo Neira: Medicine, Ideologies, and Power in the Nineteenth-Century Andes* (2001). Cloth ISBN 0-8420-2826-9 Paper ISBN 0-8420-2827-7

June E. Hahner, ed., *A Parisian in Brazil: The Travel Account of a Frenchwoman in Nineteenth-Century Rio de Janeiro* (2001). Cloth ISBN 0-8420-2854-4 Paper ISBN 0-8420-2855-2

Richard A. Warren, *Vagrants and Citizens: Politics and the Masses in Mexico City from Colony to Republic* (2001). ISBN 0-8420-2964-8

Roderick J. Barman, *Princess Isabel of Brazil: Gender and Power in the Nineteenth Century* (2002). Cloth ISBN 0-8420-2845-5 Paper ISBN 0-8420-2846-3

Stuart F. Voss, *Latin America in the Middle Period, 1750–1929* (2002). Cloth ISBN 0-8420-5024-8 Paper ISBN 0-8420-5025-6